EVIL

A Primer

A History of a
Bad Idea from Beelzebub
to Bin Laden

———————

THOMAS DUNNE BOOKS
ST. MARTIN'S PRESS
NEW YORK

EVIL

A Primer

WILLIAM HART

THOMAS DUNNE BOOKS.
An imprint of St. Martin's Press.

www.stmartins.com

Book design by Jennifer Ann Daddio

ISBN 0-312-31281-4
EAN 978-0312-31281-7

First Edition: October 2004

10 9 8 7 6 5 4 3 2 1

DISCARDED

TO JEAN DUFFY AND JIM HART,

who saw for themselves but

didn't look away

CONTENTS

ACKNOWLEDGMENTS

There are too many debts. Everybody knows something about evil, and many people know some quite remarkable things about it; I have gained a lot by listening. Like the rest of us, of course, I owe the most to the thinkers, artists, and poets whose stunning intellectual achievements so enrich our lives — and form the basis of this little book. Second, we owe the scholars whose investigations and explanations permit us access to those achievements. Then there's my brother, the relentless Jim Hart Jr., who gave me much meaty guidance, early and late. Judge Michael Wilkinson and Jack Potts, M.D., are foremost among those who lent their expertise and insights, Potts being the one who sort of started the whole thing. Of course, any misunderstandings of their input is strictly my doing. Anne Winter provided support and suggestions while also keeping the general intelligence level up. The kids — they know who they are — kept the noise level up. I was blessed with a wise and patient editor in Sean Desmond, and was rescued, Lazarus-like, from the dead by my agent, the incomparable Flip Brophy.

INTRODUCTION

———

Today our nation saw evil.

—PRES. GEORGE W. BUSH, SEPTEMBER 11, 2001

Sure we did. What happened that day was not simply misfortune, or life's inevitable downside, or the blind working out of probabilities. We all believe that it was an event different in kind, not just degree, from the world's everyday woes. It was more than merely bad, or even very, very bad. The earth moved, if slightly, beneath our feet.

It was evil.

Evil! Like a zombie back from the grave, it arose—a word many of us had long ago relegated to Sunday sermons, video games, and horror flicks. Even as it fell from our lips, it gave off a quaint, tinny sound, seemingly so out of place in an age that worships science and business and . . . maybe golf.

But of course it is not out of place. Evil is not old-fashioned, was never gone, and—depending on your religious bent—will never go away. Far from being exotic, it's among the most common elements of everyday life. Just consider how many toddlers were suffering though their private family hells when the planes hit on that Tuesday morning in September. How many grandmas were losing their savings to the nice man on the phone. How many hearts and bones were being broken. How many secret deals were being sealed with a smirk.

The 2001 World Trade Center attacks must qualify on any reasonable scale as not only evil but monstrous evil. But the more important fact is that such mind-numbing catastrophes can distract us from everyday evil that permeates our lives, and from the links between vast eruptions of wickedness and the chronic, low-level moral disorders that together pose greater challenges to our modest efforts to live well. For some reason—or for a lot of reasons—we've been conditioned to think that evil is a mysterious force that emanates from some higher (supernatural) or deeper (biological) source than we are capable of comprehending, and that trying to comprehend it is a task best left to the experts.

But consider the state of today's world: this is the work of experts?

Maybe we should rethink this. Maybe it should not take a vast catastrophe like September 11 to jolt us into dusting off the e-word. Nor should it require politicians, imams, or televangelists to inform us how to react. In fact, we all wrestle every day with what philosophers have for centuries called "the Problem of Evil." Every one of us. We can deny it, but it will surface. And we ignore it at our peril. "In keeping silent about evil," Aleksander Solzhenitsyn warned, "in burying it so deep within us that no sign of it appears on the surface, we are implanting it, and it will rise up a thousandfold in the future."

Like Plato, Augustine, Kant, and others among history's celebrity thinkers, we practice the ancient arts of metaphysical speculation and ethical disputation every damn day. We deliver ad-lib homilies to the kids, balance family against work, stomach the daily horrors in the headlines, stagger through years of guilt, choose to be merciful, flail away at the thousand choices we make as we rush along.

Then we lay head on pillow and wonder how we did.

Some people conduct their inquiries into topics like evil with compound words crafted into elaborate conceptual edifices. Some grunt, some curse. Some pray, some cry, some flee, some fight. But we cannot *not* think about evil.

True, a lot of reasonable people wince at the word because of its unsavory past. The word *evil* has a sordid history as a weapon of politics and religion, and even today it seems that those who brandish it most vigorously are the intolerant and the paranoid. But is it wise to surrender this word to those who flaunt it? Instead, maybe we should step back, sit down, and ponder evil without ranting, chanting, or rushing for the exits. God may be dead or may have departed without leaving a forwarding address; our divisions may seem to deepen. But even amid this runaway moral pluralism, most of us can readily agree that evil exists and that it seems as robust as ever.

If we can agree on that, maybe we can agree on more. Maybe we could try to get a closer look at exactly what we call "evil." Drag it out of its comfortable darkness and hold it up to the light. Maybe we could reintroduce evil to rational conversation, in the coffee line and at the dinner table. Who knows, it might at least help us get through the next terror, or through tomorrow's thousand decisions.

This little book is offered with that in mind.

It's also worth noting what this book is not. It is not an apology for wicked deeds or doers; it does not trivialize human suffering for laughs; it is not a vehicle for ridiculing anyone's spiritual beliefs; it is not an endorsement of the occult or the paranormal or, God help us, of satanism.

If anything, this is a quest. A quick search for possible answers to impossible questions. Why, as Harold Kushner famously wrote, do bad things happen to good people? Why, if evil deeds are hateful, are the consequences of evil sometimes—well—not all bad? Without evil, some thinkers insist, there could not be goodness.

Without evil, our literature would be stripped of conflict; instead of Shakespeare we'd have what—travelogues? Our music would be likewise impoverished. Good-bye, "Whipping Post," hello, "On Wisconsin!" Russian novelist Fyodor Dostoevsky wrote that without evil life would be "an endless church service; it would be holy, but tedious." We'd be terminally humorless—for what fine quip is not first dipped in malice before being flung?

Some say that without evil, without the heartbreaking price it exacts in fear, suffering, and grief, humans could never truly taste freedom.

Finally, why does evil excite us so? Everyone feels its silky lure. Most of us—maybe just that one time—have blown a Commandment, lost our way, gone too far in the blurry hours after midnight. And no wonder: Evil seduces with promises of passion and excess—of transcendence over the merely physical and rational and present. It *guarantees* perfection, as the serpent did to Eve, which is why the figures of Dracula and de Sade and Hitler and Manson not only terrify and enrage but also beckon. "Evil" may sound like an echo from a bygone, candlelit era. Yet it can still send shivers down a modern spine—shivers of fear, shivers of delight.

We should admit that we love evil too much to give it up.

—GANDHI

EVIL

A Primer

One

WHERE DO WE START?

I am the Lord, and there is none else.
I form the light, and create darkness:
I make peace, and create evil:
I the Lord do all these things.

—ISAIAH 45:6–7

The belief in a supernatural source of evil is not necessary;
men alone are quite capable of every wickedness.

—JOSEPH CONRAD

*The unique and supreme voluptuousness of love lies in the
certainty of committing evil. And men and women know
from birth that in evil is found all sensual delight.*

— CHARLES BAUDELAIRE

*No reason. No conscience. No understanding. Not even the
most rudimentary sense of life or death, good or evil, right
or wrong . . . what was living behind that boy's eyes was,
purely and simply, evil.*

— PSYCHIATRIST DESCRIBING THE YOUNG
MICHAEL MYERS, IN THE FILM *HALLOWEEN*

We begin, as we must, with humility and reverence. Not to mention a wee nervousness.
Despite five thousand years of recorded human wrongdoing, despite all that our prophets and presidents and scholars and poets and undead homicidal maniacs have told us, the origin and definition of evil remain impossible to pin down.

This is no mere historical curiosity. This is more than clever wordplay by duelling theologians. This is actually where we've ended up after centuries of seeking answers to no less a question than—as Socrates put it—"how we are to live." Socrates believed he knew the answer, and it got him the hemlock. So, on the other hand, did the Marquis de Sade and Josef Stalin and serial killer Ted Bundy—who once described the moment of murder thus: "You feel the last bit of breath leaving their body. You're looking into their eyes. A person in that situation is God!"

They all knew the answer. Inconveniently, their answers were all different.

And when it comes to evil, so are ours. True, we've long had Satan, who emerged in the New Testament as supreme cosmic villain. But while a majority of Americans still profess belief in the Prince of Darkness, for most of us he's lost his luster as a one-stop answer to questions about evil. The more closely we examine evil, in fact, the more it splinters. We've all heard "Thou shall not kill." So killing is evil? Certainly. Well, usually. Can the word *evil* be applied to a tornado that swoops down upon a grade school and leaves it a sea of bloody, broken wreckage? Our hearts cry out yes! But how can the weather be evil? It's hard to imagine a greater evil than a tiny child crushed by a car, but is it still evil if the driver didn't mean to do it?

Is it evil for a lawyer to help a guilty criminal evade punishment? For a coyote to have your cat for lunch? For CEOs to plunder corporations while balancing on the knife-edge boundaries of the law? For wealthy people to wax richer while their neighbors struggle in poverty? For a human to kill animals for sport or to perform painful experiments on our first cousin, the chimp?

Such devilishly difficult questions. A reasonable

approach to answering them might start with the *Oxford English Dictionary*, which notes that the word *evil* descends from ancient Teutonic words meaning "too much" or "over the limit." Yet the worthy *OED*'s first definition is "the opposite of Good." This is not much help; the opposite of a good cigar is not an evil one. At the other extreme is the widely cited 1964 comment by former U.S. Supreme Court justice Potter Stewart. It's tough to define hard-core pornography, the justice said, "but I know it when I see it."

In fact, it seems we find ourselves without much of a common vocabulary for collectively addressing life's greatest challenge. Evil has always been a topic of discussion on Sundays in America, but over the past two centuries the word has largely faded from common use. It's made a partial comeback with recent concerns over terrorism, but this confused furor, too, only underscores how unprepared we are to wrestle with the concept. As Andrew Delbanco put it in *The Death of Satan*, "We have no language for connecting our inner lives with the horrors that pass before our eyes in the outer world."

The old certainties still thunder forth regularly from podiums and the pulpits. But listen closely, and you'll hear evil denounced or lamented — or brandished against others — but seldom explained. Meanwhile, we inhabit a society morally confused and sharply divided over fundamental questions of right and wrong, as it is about race, poverty, abortion, homosexuality, immigration, capital punishment—to name just a few.

But despite our moral fragmentation, despite what Delbanco calls "this crisis of incompetence before evil," most of us will immediately agree that evil remains brutally real—as real today as in the time of Job or Torquemada or Vlad the Impaler. The twentieth century is commonly called the bloodiest in history. From Cambodia to Rwanda to Bosnia to the latest local headlines, our fellow humans seem capable of committing literally any outrage, of hurling themselves into unbounded savagery or treachery. How? Why? As we charge off into the third millennium, we're still being stalked by fifty centuries' worth of the same terrible questions.

Questions that must have arisen in response to *Homo sapiens*' earliest experiences of pain and loss. The clay tablets of the Sumerians, who lived five thousand years ago in what is now Iraq, and who are generally credited with the invention of writing, contain laments that seem eerily familiar to us today:

> *My companion says not a true word to me,*
> *My friend gives the lie to my righteous word,*
> *The man of deceit has conspired against me.*

Evil, in fact, may have have commanded our attention before good. Historian Paul Carus says, "There seems to be no exception to the rule that fear is always the first incentive to religious worship . . . a powerful evil deity looms up as the most important personage in the remotest past of almost every faith."

In recent centuries we've championed such explanations for wickedness as superstition, ignorance, illness, childhood trauma, social conditioning, and defective genes. But humans' earliest sense of evil was hardly so elaborate; it was likely associated simply with physical survival in a fearsome world. A catalogue of those early evils by Jungian analyst Marie-Louise von Franz included "hunger, cold, fire, landslides and avalanches, snowstorms, drowning, storms at sea, being lost in the forest, the big enemy animals, the ice bear in the north, the lion or crocodile in Africa, etc." Contemporary philosopher Amelie Rorty says our earliest notions of evil involved "abominations—acts that, like incest, cannibalism, patricide, and fratricide—elicit horror and disgust." French philosopher Paul Ricoeur says primitive humans associated evil with the idea of "defilement," a condition that itself had to be countered with some ritual of purification—all of which sounds a lot like the beginnings of humankind's primary answer to misfortune: organized religion.

At some point we began to pray to supernatural spirits to ease their anger at our apparent sins and to protest our innocence. The Egyptian Book of the Dead, dating from perhaps 2500 B.C.E., portrays newly dead souls seeking a favorable judgment from the gods by intoning long lists of the things they did *not* do, from, "I have not done falsehood against men" to, "I have not built a dam on flowing water."

As the world adopted religions with divinely inspired rules, Rorty notes, evil evolved into a sense of disobedience. Evil became sin. But why do we sin? Many cultures, especially in the Middle East but also in the West, decided early on that promoting evil is the vile work of one or more supernatural beings. The Egyptians had Seth, the lord of the desert whom the Greeks later equated with Typhon, whence the word *typhoon*. Zoroaster, the widely influential Iranian religious leader of the sixth century B.C.E., is generally credited with identifying the first being of pure evil, Angra Mainyu. The Babylonians had the nocturnal female demon Lilitu; the Israelites had Azazel and Beelzebub, among others; the ancient Germans, Loki, sire of the wolf; the Christians, Satan; and the Muslims, Iblis.

Today we have . . . Hannibal Lecter?

This celebrity-villain approach remains humans' most popular way to explain where evil comes from. Of course it's not universal: Millions of us follow creeds, chiefly Hinduism and Buddhism, that either pack the stage with villains or dismiss them all as B-list poseurs. More about that in the next chapter.

But the leaders of the young Christian church also developed another approach to defining evil, this one by focusing on what it's *not*. This ended with the surprising conclusion that evil does not exist. You read that right. Plato and his later interpreters had defined evil as falling so low on the scale of existence that it registers as a negative, as "nonbeing." This idea fit well with the Christians' urgent need to explain how evil could exist in a world created by a single, all-loving God. Augustine, the fifth-century North African thinker who so powerfully shaped Christian doctrine, concluded that evil cannot exist—cannot have "being"—in such a cosmos, but must be seen only as the absence of good, or *privatio boni*. To skeptics, this adroit explanation might sound more worthy of Bill Clinton than of a Church Father, but it helped form the foundation of Christian dogma. One especially florid expression of it came from a Syrian monk commonly referred to by the remarkable name of Pseudo-Dionysius the Areopagite. Around 500 he wrote: "[Evil is] a lack, a deficiency, a weakness, a disproportion, an error, purposeless, unlovely, lifeless, unwise, unreasonable, imperfect, unreal, causeless, indeterminate, sterile, inert, powerless, disordered, incongruous, indefinite, dark, unsubstantial, and never in itself possessed of any existence whatever."

You get the idea. Over the centuries, the Christian Church gradually consolidated its power and its doctrines concerning evil and settled in to battle Satan for the souls of humankind. It also battled Islam, which arose in seventh-century Arabia, even though Islam also preaches the story of Adam and Eve and blames evil on Satan, or Iblis, an angel cast down because of pride. Then, as Mark Larrimore of Princeton writes, came three tectonic historial shifts that wrought monumental changes in our view of evil. First was the Renaissance, usually dated from the fourteenth to the seventeenth centuries, during which humans' focus moved from the afterlife to the life of this world. Evil and suffering, Larrimore says, were less easily explained away with refer ences to cosmic mysteries, because "most people today are unimpressed by the insignificance of this life in comparison with eternity."

Second was the Enlightenment, the eighteenth-century philosophical movement that questioned reigning values and beliefs—notably including Adam's fall and original sin. That, Larrimore notes, undermined the long-standing Christian (Though not Muslim) doctrine that humans *deserved* to suffer in this world because they were already tainted by evil at birth. This naturally raised the question: if we don't *have* to suffer, why are we suffering?

We're still wrestling with that one.

Third, Larrimore suggests, came the impact of modern medicine and its dramatic reduction of pain and loss. "The problem of evil became acute," he says, ". . . once suffering no longer seemed a necessary part of life, but exceptional."

Exceptional, but not gone. Rationalism and science may have led us out of the dank gloom of superstition, but they also shredded the Christian West's once broad and stable beliefs in the origins of evil—then stopped there. They've certainly not banished evil and ushered in utopia, as Karl Marx and other infectious dreamers confidently predicted they would. So where are we left? Evil undeniably thrives, while science denies us any cosmic explanation to salve our wounds or guide us to shelter. This is progress?

Much of the fault appears to be our own. As science nicely explains away so many of our traditional terrors, we cling ever more tightly to others—what's up with those crop circles, anyway?—and discover later-model demons who ride UFOs instead of broomsticks. We seem almost to want evil lurking in our cognitive shadows like a storybook vampire avoiding the sun; content to glimpse it out of the corner of our eye, we seldom try to see its face.

Even Hollywood, so often condemned as the enemy of righteous, God-fearing society, turns out to be a major ally. From Dracula to Darth Vader, horror flicks have only reinforced our deep-rooted belief in evil as a mysterious force unleashed by the violation of some code that ultimately derives from the divine. True, *Bride of Chucky* is no *Paradise Lost*, but the underlying moral lessons are the same. The French poet Charles Baudelaire famously remarked that the Devil's greatest trick was to convince us he doesn't exist. Hollywood, *au contraire,* toils faithfully to assure us that he does.

Why? Because Hollywood knows that evil attracts us, even in little doses. Sociologist Jack Katz quotes a shoplifter: "Once outside the door I thought Wow! I pulled it off, I faced danger and I pulled it off. I was smiling so much and I felt at that moment like there was nothing I couldn't do."

Most of us can at least imagine the thrill of violating a law or a taboo. Usually, of course, we're thinking about minor transgressions that we amiably label "vices," rather than extreme cases in which we've "thirsted after the bliss of the knife," as Friedrich Nietzsche put it. Augustine himself lamented how, at age sixteen, he and some other kids stole pears from a neighbor's tree just to do it. "Foul was the evil, and I loved it," he wrote. "I loved to go down to death. I loved my fault, not that for which I did the fault, but I loved my fault itself."

Now that's guilt. True believers like Augustine easily explain our liking for evil as arising from the foul doings of Satan or his henchmen. Nonbelievers have to explain why we set up moral rules—against theft, adultery, tailgating—that we then lust to break. One popular answer is to locate the problem in biological rules that some scientists believe directly underlie our moral ones. Evolutionary psychologists, as we'll see in chapter 4, contend that our traditionally defined "evils" are little more than manifestations of embedded human survival urges like lust, greed, and aggression.

To confuse things even more, there's our long-standing recognition that, well, evil isn't all bad.

Plotinus, a highly influential Neoplatonist philosopher of the third century, noted: "Vice itself has many useful sides: it brings about much that is beautiful, in artistic creations for example, and it stirs us to thoughtful living, not allowing us to drowse in security." Other thinkers old and new have linked man's rebellious instincts to the precious goal of freedom: "This first fact of disobedience," psychoanalyst Erich Fromm wrote, "is man's first step toward freedom." French Renaissance essayist Michel de Montaigne went further: "Whoever would take away the knowledge and sense of evil, would, at the same time, eradicate the sense of pleasure, and, in short, annihilate man himself."

Georg Friedrich Hegel, the influential nineteenth-century German philosopher, went even further, linking evil to the emergence of human consciousness and individuality from the primitive soup of animal instincts: "Evil lies in consciousness: for the [animals] are neither evil nor good. . . . Consciousness occasions the separation of the ego, in its boundless freedom as arbitrary choice, from the pure essence of the will."

Theories about why evil attracts as well as repels us have filled many volumes and will be touched upon throughout this one. Surely most of us avert our eyes, and our rationality, from evil because we've been taught to do so, and warned that staring too long at the dark side is highly dangerous—a lesson embodied in the Greek myth of Medusa. But the see-no-evil approach hasn't worked very well. Worse, it may even hinder us from understanding evil by confusing two critically different senses of the word:

In the first sense, *evil* simply means the extremely bad things that happen, from war to crime to Reality TV. Surely we can all agree—OK, not the Buddhists—that empirical evil is an authentic part of everyday life.

In the second sense, the word is defined according to the myth or ideology that a group or society adopts, cherishes, and mercilessly defends. It is here that religion enters, rationality is trumped by revelation, and agreement disintegrates.

Lust, cruelty, greed—examples of evil in the first sense have been constants of human existence from Cain to Al Capone. But the ways in which we address them—our ideologies of evil—have undergone staggering transformations. Listen, for one small example, to this judgment pronounced by a court in Avignon, France, in 1542, during the European witch frenzy that dispatched thousands to unspeakable torture and death:

> *Taught by [Beelzebub], you ... did murder many new-born children, and with the help of that old serpent Satan you did*

afflict mankind with curses, loss of milk, the wasting sickness, and other most grave diseases. And with your own children . . . you did with those magic spells suffocate, pierce and kill, and finally you dug them up secretly by night from the cemetery, where they were buried, and so carried them to . . . the Prince of Devils sitting upon his throne.

What universe was that? Most historians now tell us that the widespread and terrifying "evil" of witchcraft was fictional (though the evil done in response was surely real). The ideology, in other words, overcame and shaped the reality. Now compare that passage to the dry machine-prose prized by today's popular—and also fictional—cop and court shows, where even the most savage and grotesque crimes are rendered in clipped "forensic" language that strips evil of its mystery and even its horror. At least the latter is modeled on real evil.

But that doesn't seem to matter. The sixteenth-century passage openly reflects our deeply embedded human belief in what philosopher Paul Ricoeur called the "substance-force of evil": Early peoples, according to Ricoeur, thought of evil as "a quasi-material something that infects as a sort of filth, that harms by invisible properties, and that nevertheless works in the manner of a force in the field of our undividedly psychic and corporeal existence." And despite the Renaissance and the Enlightenment and our modern penchant for

Dragnet-speak, this ideology of evil still thrives. From pastors to ethical pundits like William Bennett to every teenage Marilyn Manson fan, many or most modern Americans still think of evil as a mysterious, malicious force. It appears as a sly, shadowy presence, a demonic spell, the ineffable workings of a cosmic balance wheel, something crouching out there just beyond the light of the campfires.

These are breathtaking visions. This is precisely what demands the elaborate, ritualistic death that always befalls the obvious slut and the wiseass guy in teenage slasher flicks; and dammit, we're glad it does. But is this how real evil happens? Uh, no, notes philosopher Nel Noddings:

> *[Encountering real evil,] we feel none of the excitement conveyed by stories of devils, witches, demons, spells and possession. Evil does not have a stomach-turning stench, nor does it signal its presence with palpable cold and darkness. We do not fall into it, haplessly, nor does it entrap [possess] us.*

That doesn't make for much of a nightmare, on Elm Street or anywhere else. But face it: few of us have actually encountered, say, a hobgoblin. And when evil things befall us—an assault, a betrayal by a friend, a crippling financial loss, the death of a loved one—spooky special effects are seldom involved. As we'll see in chapter 5, philosopher Hannah Arendt famously spoke of "the banality of evil." And Noddings cites French political activist Simone Weil's description of actual evil as "gloomy, monotonous, barren, boring."

So which is it? Is evil best understood as a dark supernatural force emanating from unknowable mysteries lost in the primeval mists of history? Or is it just a collective name for the ugly, bad stuff that . . . happens? How best can we choose among Sunday-school evil and Hollywood evil and textbook evil and psychic-fair evil and fairy-tale evil and crime-scene evil and even talk-show evil? ("She's sleeping with his gay brother!")

Nobody yet has successfully disposed of this centuries-old issue in a few pages, or even in a lot of pages. But perhaps we can come up with a bare working definition. Wisdom suggests a minimalist approach.

In general, scholars tend to cite four choices for the source of evil: 1) humans through their actions, 2) the natural condition of the universe, 3) supernatural demons, 4) a god or gods. Let's review a few approaches, plain and fancy:

- Plato, who called God's world "the fairest of creations," did not blame the Creator for evil. Instead, he seemed to see evil as the result of naturally occurring human feelings, like love, fear, and anger, that have grown out of control and "conquered" a person.
- For something completely different, consider the

fifth-century Indian teacher Siddhartha Gotama, the Buddha, who taught that evil is an illusion (the good news) because all of existence is suffering (the bad news) caused by our erroneous belief in our individual identities.

- Augustine, arguably history's most influential Christian theologian, taught that evil is the act of turning away from God, "for when the will abandons what is above itself, and turns to what is lower, it becomes evil—not because that is evil to which it turns, but because the turning itself is wicked."

- In the fourteenth-century *Canterbury Tales,* Geoffrey Chaucer provides the classic medieval definition of evil as sin, based on the original sin we inherited from Adam through the "vile and corrupt matter" of the flesh. Chaucer cites the Seven Deadly Sins: pride, "the general root of all evils"; envy; anger; melancholia (sloth); avarice—"the eagerness of the heart to have earthly things"; gluttony; and lechery.

- In *Paradise Lost,* seventeenth-century English poet John Milton further enshrined the dominant Christian teaching that it was Satan's sin of pride that gave rise to evil—or to "Misery, uncreated till the crime of thy Rebellion."

- In contrast, French Enlightenment philosopher Jean-Jacques Rousseau—who believed humans

originally existed as "noble savages" in a "state
of nature"—saw evil as the corruption of this
natural purity. "God makes all things good; man
meddles with them and they become evil."

- Writing about Shakespeare's classic villain Iago
in 1818, Samuel Taylor Coleridge famously noted
the "motive-hunting of motiveless Malignity. . . .
A being next to Devil—only not quite Devil."

- For Karl Marx, the Devil as well as the Lord
was merely in the way. Evil arises from the
unjust power relationships imposed upon human
beings by history—relationships that will
inevitably be swept away.

- Friedrich Nietzsche, the controversial
nineteenth-century scholar and philosopher who
described himself as "philosophizing with a hammer," denounced conventional notions of evil as
repressive tools of the "slave morality" of Christianity, which he said caused suffering by opposing humans' natural, noble instincts towards
power, freedom, pleasure, and achievement.

- Sigmund Freud associated evil with Thanatos, the
"death instinct," the natural seat of aggression in
humans and the counterweight to Eros, the drive
towards sex, life, and love. "Those who love fairy-
tales," he wrote, "do not like it when people speak
of the innate tendencies in mankind towards
aggression, destruction, and, in addition, cruelty."

- Carl Jung associated human evil with the Shadow, the dark side of an individual's personality—the side that promotes anger, lust, and deceit. We unconsciously "project" the Shadow, with all its hateful, threatening qualities, onto others—whom we then see as evil.
- Erich Fromm wrote that evil as well as good human passions "can be understood only as a person's attempt to make sense of his life and transcend banal, merely life-sustaining existence."
- Contemporary historian Jeffrey Burton Russell says, "Evil is meaningless, senseless destruction. . . . The essence of evil is abuse of a sentient being, a being that can feel pain."
- Contemporary psychiatrist and author M. Scott Peck believes "evil can be defined as a specific form of mental illness." It might, he says, be best compared to a condition called "ambulatory schizophrenia," and it is marked by "consistent, destructive, scapegoating behavior"; intolerance of criticism; exaggerated concern with a public image of respectability; and "intellectual deviousness."

Quite a mix. Now what?

First, let's agree that evil does indeed exist. Meaning that bad things do happen to good people. This is no joke: a good argument can be made that evil does not exist—and not only by Buddhists. This argument maintains that the label "evil" is so subjective as to be meaningless, except as a way for some people—usually political or religious leaders—to slander some and control others.

But the extreme savagery of human behavior does seem to cry out for special attention. Why should we not call such behavior "evil," so long as we take care not to then rush thoughtlessly into a jihad or another sequel to *Hellraiser*? We may not agree on which impulses or actions are evil, but we can agree that evil does exist.

Second, let's limit evil to acts performed by humans. The massive earthquake that leveled western Indian cities in February 2001, burying thousands alive, caused immense suffering to innocent people. Was it evil? For centuries many people regarded such occurrences as evil; the Old Testament is packed with storms and plagues dispatched as punishment by a wrathful Yahweh. Philosopher Susan Neiman, in *Evil in Modern Thought*, notes the devastating psychic impact of the 1755 Lisbon earthquake on Europe. But science has severely undermined this view. Earthquakes, hurricanes, and other destructive natural events are now typically set aside by philosophers as "nonmoral" or "natural" evil because they don't violate moral codes or feature anybody to blame. Let's do likewise.

Third, let's limit our discussion to intentional acts. Many evildoers justify their actions with some variation of "the devil made me do it," and we commonly punish destructive acts even if the actor—say, a drunk driver who causes a fatal accident—didn't intend to hurt anyone. Arendt, as we shall see, created a haunting portrait of real evil occurring without real villains, and this is a vision we will confront. But throughout history it's been the intentional evildoer, the Iago, who poses the most troubling questions.

Fourth, remember the title of Rabbi Kushner's best-seller, *When Bad Things Happen to Good People*? Now consider the converse: some people do ask for it. They *deserve* to be assaulted, or ripped off, or tricked, or abandoned, or otherwise harmed. Few of us, for example, would condemn the Germans who vainly sought to assassinate Hitler—or a police sting that tricks felons into capture. The victims of true evil must be people who don't deserve it.

Fifth, let's agree that evil is an impulse or act whose results are more than just bad, or even *very* bad. Philosophers seeking universal definitions may include as "evil" anything that interferes even slightly with humans' universal desire to lead happy lives. But this leaves us laymen with a definition too broad to be of practical use. For us, evil's effects must be profound, widespread, long-lasting, or all three. Cutting ahead in line is bad, as are littering, auto theft, and slander; but if we deem these evil, what do we call genocide?

Sixth, we must quiet our minds a moment and place

hands on hearts. Most of us feel an almost physical blow at hearing of, say, "ethnic cleansing" or the sexual abuse of a child. It seizes us. This wave of awe, nausea, and horror cannot be ignored in identifying evil, which manifests itself to the viscera as well as to the mind. In an important, if not absolute, sense, we do "know it when we see it."

Seventh, evil acts worthy of the name victimize others besides their obvious victims; they injure us all. Consider the looting of a corporation, the torture of a prisoner. Such acts seem more than just crimes; they are assaults upon our ethical order, eroding the possibility of trust and shaking our faith in human goodness.

Finally, let's keep it simple. It's tempting to conjure up elaborate, airtight definitions—we've already waded through a few—but it's a bit early in our inquiry for such heroics. Instead, borrowing from philosopher John Kekes and others, let's start with the basics: evil is an intentional human act that causes extreme harm to innocents and attacks our basic moral order.

Hardly poetic. Not scary. And wait—where does God come in? That's what we'll look at next. Meanwhile, if you're feeling a little unsatisfied, a little let down, remember you're in good company: At least five thousand years' worth.

Two

LAZARUS!
COME OUT!

Whoever admits that anything living is evil must either believe that God is malignantly capable of creating evil, or else believe that God has made many mistakes.

—GEORGE BERNARD SHAW

God therefore neither wills evil to be done, nor wills it not to be done, but wills to permit evil to be done; and this is a good.

—THOMAS AQUINAS

Religion is the sigh of the oppressed creature, the heart of a heartless world. . . . It is the opium of the people.

—KARL MARX

However we end up defining evil, history tells us that men and women of every epoch have turned primarily to religion to ease the pains of mortality and its grim handmaidens—fear, disease, loss. Surely even the most scrupulous atheist would admit that faith in a supernatural order has through the centuries brought much peace to suffering humans, as well as much suffering.

Just imagine, for example, history's uncounted multitudes of nameless slaves and widows and peasants and prisoners and lost children and terrified soldiers trembling in some long-forgotten black night. Then imagine them drifting off into the gentlest of sleeps with a cherished icon pressed to their hearts. Who would begrudge them that? Who can deny feeling at least the faintest stirring of hope at Jesus' glorious proclamation of faith's victory over death itself: "I am the resurrection and the life. If anyone believes in me, even though he dies he will live, and whoever lives and believes in me will never die." Then, the Gospel of John tells us, Jesus had the stone rolled back from the tomb. "He cried in a loud voice, 'Lazarus, here! Come out!' The dead man came out, his feet and hands bound with bands of stuff and a cloth round his face."

That's it, right there. The hope of immortality is what we humans have craved ever since we fled the first snarling beast or cringed in terror before the first lightning bolt. And religion has supplied it longer and more persuasively than any other human enterprise. And despite its decline in recent centuries, it still does, especially in the United States. Polls consistently record the vast majority of Americans—90 percent or more— calling themselves believers, with well over half terming religion "very important" in their lives.

And even these healthy numbers pale before the level of faith sustained by human beings thoughout most of our history. Concerning medieval Europe, for example, historian Lucien Febvre notes: "One was Christian in fact. . . . Whether one wanted to be or not, whether one clearly understood or not, one found oneself immersed from birth in a bath of Christianity from which one did not emerge even at death." Even nineteenth-century America was so drenched in religion that Michael Shaara, author of the Pulitzer Prize–winning *Killer Angels*, felt compelled to update the language in Civil War soldiers' letters because of the extreme "religiosity" of the time. Then again, taking part in Pickett's charge—which was less a charge than a brisk march into a firing squad—might bring out the religiosity in anyone.

Still, the question must be asked: have all these centuries of fervent belief actually conquered evil, or banished it, or at least driven it back deep onto its own side of the field? In concrete terms, the evidence isn't encouraging: a glance out the window confirms that wickedness continues to thrive. Billions still live in poverty, the strong exploit the weak, villains prosper, the Yankees keep winning, and so on. And a closer look reveals an even more critical crack in religion's armor against the world's woes. The inconvenient fact is that, for most of us—that is, for the planet's Christians, Muslims, and Jews—the very existence of evil renders faith in God not only questionable but even— there's really no other word—nonsensical.

Here's why. If we seek refuge from evil in one all-loving, all-powerful God—Yahweh, Allah, God the Father, the Great Goddess, whomever—we can't avoid facing one spectacularly awkward question: why does God permit evil in the first place? Being all-powerful, why didn't God create a world just like ours but without evil, or at least without the worst extremes of human savagery—no serial sexual predators, say, and no English soccer fans?

Evil's very presence on the planet hurls a lethal challenge at our faith in God's goodness and power and, ultimately, at His very existence. Welcome to what philosophers call, with deceptive mildness, the "Problem of Evil."

It's hardly a mild problem. Fyodor Dostoevsky wrote: "Listen! If all must suffer to pay for [God's] eternal harmony, what have children to do with it, tell me, please? It's beyond all comprehension why they should suffer, and why they should pay for the harmony."

True, many believers today counter such laments with the reponse that the modern age's challenge to religion is nothing more than Satan's work, manifested in the corrosive effects of secular society. Prominent Baptist minister Jerry Falwell articulated this conviction in his remarks following the terrorist attacks of September 11, 2001:

I really believe that the pagans, and the abortionists, and the feminists, and the gays and the lesbians who are actively trying to make that an alternative lifestyle . . . all of them who have tried to secularize America. I point the finger in their face and say, "You made this happen."

Falwell's remarks raised a furor, but they surely reflected the views of millions of Americans who consider themselves evangelical or born-again Christians, and who equate evil with enmity to their religion — or at least with enmity to their religion. This is certainly true to the mainstream Christian tradition, which regards evil as an offense against God. Indeed, the culture wars in the United States are a clash between competing explanations for evil — for the moral degradation both sides see around us. Some believers trace the baleful effects of secularization further back in time, citing the skepticism fanned by the eighteenth-century Enlightenment or the rise of socialism or even the theory of evolution. These are not idle arguments: Charles Darwin, a good Christian gentleman, was shaken by his own findings. "I am bewildered," he wrote in 1860 in response to the furor kicked up by his *Origin of Species by Means of Natural Selection,* published the preceding year. "I had no intention to write atheistically."

On the other hand, Darwin went on to write: "there seems to me too much misery in the world. I cannot persuade myself that a beneficent and omnipotent God would have designedly created the Ichneumonidae [wasps] with the express intention of their feeding within the living bodies of Caterpillars, or that a cat should play with mice."

So much for Tom and Jerry. In fact, evil's challenge to faith didn't start in the nineteenth century or even the ninth, but is probably as old as human history. Epicurus, an ancient Greek philosopher who lived during the time of Aristotle and Alexander the Great, is widely credited with an early logical formulation of this haunting dilemma:

> *God is all-powerful.*
> *God is perfectly good.*
> *Evil exists.*
> *If God exists, there would be no evil.*
> *Therefore, God does not exist.*

This is more than theological trash talk. No less an authority than Thomas Aquinas, the towering thirteenth-century Christian scholar, considered this dilemma the greatest challenge to faith. And here's English philosopher David Hume, writing nineteen centuries after Epicurus:

> *Is [God] willing to prevent evil, but not able?*
> *then is he impotent. Is he able, but not willing?*
> *then is he malevolent. Is he both able and willing?*
> *whence then is evil?*

Or, in Nel Noddings's concise modern rendition, we must ask, "What sort of god would deliberately create a world in which his creatures must eat one another to live?"

Of course, the Problem of Evil does not loom as large for all souls on earth. A huge sector of humankind spared the worst are pantheists—they believe in more than one god. They don't have to explain the ways of a single all-powerful, all-good Supreme Being. Now, our inquiry must be limited to America and the West, and any effort to summarize Eastern belief systems such as Hinduism and Buddhism would be laughable. To start with, there's the question of whether it's even valid to use the blanket term *Hinduism* to cover the scores of often unrelated and even contradictory creeds and movements that have swept over the Indian subcontinent during the past four thousand years. Another problem: some deny that Buddhism in its pure form qualifies as a "religion" at all.

Still, it is worth noting that Hinduism, which recognizes scores of gods, views evil and suffering as part of the natural universe, a mechanism for keeping the world in balance. "Were all men to become virtuous, or all demons godly—there would be no universe at all," scholar Wendy O'Flaherty writes, "for there would be no 'contrasting pairs.'" Hinduism also contains the belief that the universe was created in a faulty manner, and that ritual acts can counter or repair the evil of the human condition. This idea gradually expanded to the broader doctrine of Karma, which states that the consequences of all acts, not just ritual ones, have an impact on the actor's fortunes in a future life. Some scholars point to Karma as the most logical and elegant solution to the Problem of Evil. But it's worth asking: how much comfort is there, really, in hearing that your suffering is your fault?

Siddhartha Gotama, born in northeastern India around the fifth century B.C.E., grew up in the Hindu tradition and accepted the ideas of reincarnation and Karma. But this teacher, revered as the Buddha, rejected the idea of selfhood. He taught that evil and suffering are based on attachment (to material possessions, to social status, to pleasure, to happiness), which itself is based on desire. Desire, in its turn, is provoked by ignorance or illusion, the basic illusion being that each of us is a separate, permanent being apart from the rest of existence. As long as we cling to this illusion, we will suffer.

Buddhism—or at least its practices—has gained some ground in America in recent decades. But it's hard to see how its core doctrines of selflessness, "not-doing," and antimaterialism can gain broad appeal in our modern West.

Meanwhile, billions of Christians, Muslims, and Jews have spent centuries struggling to reconcile evil with monotheistic divinity. So how have they done it?

Plato disposed of the problem by concluding that God was all-good but not all-powerful:

> *Then God, if he be good, is not the author of all things, as the many assert, but he is the cause of a few things only, and not of most things that occur to men. . . . The good is to be attributed to God alone; of the evils the causes are to be sought elsewhere, and not in him.*

But Plato, of course, was a pagan. Dualism is another response to the Problem of Evil; it has demonstrated great popularity and staying power. Dualistic religions have one god who's the source of good and another who's the source of evil. The good god can be all-good, but he cannot be not all-powerful. He means well, but sometimes falls short. Thus the good god did not create evil and cannot eliminate it, because evil is championed by another god of equal or at least considerable power.

Historians commonly cite the seventh-century B.C.E. Persian religious teacher Zoroaster—also called Zarathushtra—as a major architect of dualism. Zoroaster, whom few today ever heard of but whose doctrines influenced the world for centuries, taught that the creator god, Ahura Mazda, is countered by an independent, though less powerful, god of evil named Angra Mainyu. If Angra Mainyu sounds suspiciously like Satan, it's no coincidence; scholars believe our Devil was modeled in part on this vile predecessor.

Another famous strain of dualism was Gnosticism, which flourished as an offshoot and rival of mainstream Christianity, mainly during the second and third centuries; Gnostic texts were discovered in the late 1940s and early 1950s in Israel among the Dead Sea Scrolls. Gnosticism—more a group of related sects than a distinct religion—sharply divided existence into realms of good and evil, light and darkness. Its adherents believed that evil and suffering arise as inevitable elements of the corrupt material world—a world that includes our physical bodies. Our souls, created in another, purer world, are temporarily held captive in the present world. Only by rejecting the material world can we realize our true nature and return to a blissful existence—a teaching Gnostics considered one of Jesus' main messages.

A third prominent dualistic religious system was Manichaeism, named for the third-century Mesopotomian teacher Mani. Manichaeism at one time had adherents from China to Europe, and it was revived in Europe in the Middle Ages. Mani also taught that matter is evil and darkness, ruled by the demon he called Ahriman, while the good god Ohrmazd is the spirit of light that will in the end defeat evil and liberate the imprisoned souls.

But this sort of two-sided solution doesn't work for Christians, Muslims, and Jews. These faiths are not dualistic because Satan, while an immensely powerful agent of evil, was himself created by God and is nowhere near His equal. God will win in the end—as detailed at length in the Bible's Book of Revelation, and now at even greater length in Tim LaHaye's Left Behind series, which has sold some 50 million copies.

For Christians, in fact, the Problem of Evil has proven so daunting that it long ago spawned its own branch of theology. This field is called "theodicy," a word coined by the eighteenth-century German philosopher Gottfried Leibniz and defined in *Webster's* as the "defense of God's goodness and omnipotence in view of the existence of evil." Long before Leibniz, of course, Augustine had concluded that, because an all-good God created and controls everything, human suffering must be merely God's punishment for humans' evil deeds or otherwise a necessary, if mysterious, element in God's overall plan of perfection. This argument, still current today, has always been vulnerable to a few commonsense objections. For example, if our evil deeds actually form part of God's overall plan, why should we not just let ourselves go and plunge headlong into vice and wickedness? And given that Satan was created by an all-good God, is Satan also somehow good?

Over the centuries, monotheistic believers wrestling with the Problem of Evil have come up with numerous theodicies, but a few major themes have prevailed:

- The "free-will defense" states that an all-good, all-powerful God permits evil to exist because eliminating it would rob humans of their most precious gift, free will. We humans are free moral agents who cause most evil ourselves. God doesn't relish our suffering, but in a sense stops Himself from intervening so as to preserve our freedom from His power—much as a loving parent might. Critics of this view note, first, that even though humans doubtless bring much evil upon themselves, life is by no means fair: the distribution of suffering too often has little or nothing to do with our behavior. Sigmund Freud dryly noted: "It is by no means the rule that virtue is rewarded and wickedness punished, but it happens often enough that the violent, the crafty, and the unprincipled seize the desirable goods of the earth for themselves, while the pious go empty away." Secondly, critics might accept the principle of what we might today call "tough love," yet ask what sort of parent would stand by as her child, having done nothing wrong and barely even understanding events, suffers the tortures of starvation, abandonment, disease, or other common horrors. Surely, as Dostoevsky's Ivan Karamazov lamented, God, being all-powerful and creative beyond all our paltry human imaginings, could have created a world in which the worst evils only befall those who clearly deserve it, or where we choose freely yet never choose evil.

But God chose not to.

- Another theodicy, referred to as the "soul-making" approach, is sometimes traced back to the third-century Christian teacher Irenaeus. This view holds that God permits evil because humans require the challenge of suffering to grow morally and spiritually as they approach their ultimate goal of a more intimate relationship with Him. If we all still lived in the Garden of Eden, we could never really have the occasion to exercise our free will in significant ways and thus grow in moral stature. Those who object to this view point again to the fact that so many bad

things happen to good people, while evildoers
thrive: what lesson are we learning here? It's
also apparent, critics say, that suffering is as
likely to drive us to do evil as it is to fortify our
characters.

- Another might be called the "celestial payoff"
approach: True, suffering does seem so often to
befall innocents, but they will be compensated a
thousandfold in the afterlife. Long the fuel—one
of the fuels—of festive Irish wakes, this view has
more recently sprung to popular attention in the
wake of suicidal terrorist attacks by Muslim
extremists who seek guaranteed paradise in
exchange for martyrdom. In fact, a debate rages
within the Muslim world over this interpretation
of the Qur'an, especially concerning the provision
of "dark-eyed virgins" for the martyrs in paradise;
even more alarming, a respected German scholar
has recently argued that the Qur'an actually
promises "white raisins" instead of virgins. In
any case, however appealing—and however
comforting—a heavenly reward might sound,
most of us today are simply not prepared to
accept this blind-faith proposition. This may be
because while in past centuries it was the norm to
discount this world as merely a way station on the
journey to the afterlife, today most people seek
fulfillment before, rather than after, they die.

- Finally, there's the rather unfortunately named "unknown-purpose defense." This states that humans are humble creatures who can only—as St. Paul famously put it—"see through a glass, darkly." We are no better able to understand God's ways—in this case, the infliction of apparently pointless suffering—than an infant is able to understand his parents' ways. We were made to endure. This may seem weak advice to modern Americans geared to demand concrete solutions to evils ranging from international terrorism to unwanted body hair.

The unquestioning endurance of suffering has always held a high place in religion's response to evil, as illustrated so powerfully in the Book of Job, perhaps the Bible's premier presentation of how bad things happen to good people. Job, you'll recall, was a "a sound and honest man who feared God and shunned evil." But one day Satan—at this point still part of God's court—baited the Lord by claiming that Job was only good because God favored him with prosperity; if God took that away, Satan claimed, Job would curse him to his face. So God—almost casually, it seems in the story—agreed to let Satan torment Job just to test his faith. Many readers might stop here to ask why an all-powerful, all-loving Deity is behaving like a bored mob boss, but let's move on.

Satan did what he does best. He killed Job's many servants and stole his 7,000 sheep, 500 yoke of oxen, 3,000 camels, and 500 donkeys. He next killed Job's seven sons and three daughters, and "struck Job down with malignant ulcers from the sole of his foot to the top of his head."

In response, Job didn't retain counsel, hit the morning talk shows, or even reconsider his mode of worship; he endured. In fact, the Bible says, he triumphed over evil because he accepted his suffering, refused to turn away from God, and achieved a deeper appreciation of how God's power dwarfs that of humans.

He was wise to do so: Yahweh answers Job with several pages of celestial chest-thumping:

> *Where were you when I laid the earth's foundations? Tell me, since you are so well-informed! Who decided the dimensions of it, do you know? Or who stretched the measuring line across it? Who supports its pillars at their bases? Who laid its cornerstone when all the stars of the morning were singing with joy and the Sons of God in chorus were chanting praise?*

In the end, Yahweh rewarded Job's faith by restoring and expanding his wealth, sent in a second crew of sons and daughters, and granted Job a life span of 140 years. But, after all that, the Supreme Being still does not reveal why he permitted evil to savage Job—or the rest of us. The moral: Humans cannot possibly understand God's ways, and they had best not try.

Theodicy—while often incomprehensible—remains a remarkable monument to human faith and ingenuity. The problem, of course, is that, once unleashed, our rational, inquiring minds are relentless. It's hard—some would say impossible—to know when to stop asking why. Which means that theodicy's exquisite explanations of life's deepest mysteries are too easily undermined by the same kind of intellectual processes that created them.

But let's say that wasn't so. Say we all accepted one or more ways of reconciling faith with evil. Religion would still have one major drawback in qualifying as the answer and antidote to the world's wickedness: flipping though any history book suggests that religion has caused as much evil and suffering as it's eased. Remember those uncounted, nameless, terrified soldiers crying out in the night? Lots of them were out there fighting and killing in the name of some glorious and benevolent deity.

The Old Testament is famous for bloodbaths that make a Hollywood slasher flick look like the Teletubbies. For example, following Israel's victory over Midian, Moses was enraged with his commanders. Why? They had stopped after only killing every Midianite male, executing the five Midianite kings, plundering all their cattle, sheep, and belongings, burning down "the towns where they lived and all their encampments," and bringing back all the Midianite women and young children as captives. A thorough job, but apparently not quite cruel enough. Moses gave these orders to his officers: "Kill all the male children. Kill also all the women who have slept with a man. Spare the lives only of the young girls who have not slept with a man, and take them for yourselves."

Yahweh ruled even his chosen people with an approach that's been called an "ethics of terror." God said: "[If you disobey,] I will wreak misery upon you, consumption and fever, which cause the eyes to pine and the body to languish. . . . And if for all that you do not obey me, I will make your skies like iron and your earth like copper . . . your land shall not yield its produce."

Not exactly a group hug. In the New Testament, Jesus may have urged his followers to turn the other cheek, but many of them seemed to do just the opposite, towards each other as well as the outside world. From the earliest internal struggles among Jewish and emerging Christian sects, writes historian Elaine Pagels, "[Christians] have . . . identified their opponents, whether Jews, pagans, or heretics, with forces of evil, and so with Satan." Pagels says further:

> *Nor have things improved since. The blood-soaked history*
> *of persecution, torture, murder and destruction perpe-*
> *trated in the name of religion is difficult to grasp, let*

alone summarize, from the slaughter of Christians to the Crusades to the Inquisition to the Reformation to the European witchcraze to colonialization to today's bitter conflict in the Middle East.

Indeed, nowhere is religion's role in promoting rather than reducing evil more starkly on display today than in the Israeli-Palestinian conflict. There seems little inclination on either side to "turn the other cheek"—and indeed neither Judaism nor Islam stresses passivity in the face of violence. The Bible famously orders equal payback: "eye for eye, tooth for tooth." The Qur'an doesn't order it, but certainly permits it:

Therein we decreed for them a life for a life, an eye for an eye, a nose for a nose, an ear for an ear, a tooth for a tooth, and a wound for a wound. But if a man charitably forbears from retaliation, his remission shall atone for him.

It's difficult to find much charitable forbearance on either side in the Middle East, which is so often what happens when you combat evil with God on your side. But wait, which side *is* God on? Is it too much to ask that the Deity make his preferences just a little clearer to his suffering creatures?

Apparently it is. Which is why religion's answer to evil, why the hope raised by Jesus' glorious victory over death, has ultimately fallen short. No one has said this better than the fugitive killer known as the Misfit, in Flannery O'Connor's classic story "A Good Man Is Hard to Find":

Jesus was the only One that ever raised the dead . . . and He shouldn't have done it. He thrown everything off balance. If He did what He said, then it's nothing for you to do but throw away everything and follow Him, and if He didn't, then it's nothing for you to do but enjoy the few minutes you got left the best way you can — by killing somebody or burning down his house or doing some other meanness to him.

So which will it be? Humans' ultimate heartbreak, the Misfit tells us, is that we are born desperate to know whether God can truly defeat evil and death, yet we can never know. "I wisht I had of been there [at Lazarus's tomb]. It ain't right I wasn't there because if I had of been there I would of known . . . if I had of been there I would of known and I wouldn't be like I am now."

But here we are now, still wondering whether Lazarus actually did walk out of that cave, "his feet and hands bound with bands of stuff and a cloth round his face." We are still struggling to reconcile the existence of evil with that of a good God. But if religion's performance has been, well, mixed, it has at least provided one spectacular answer to evil that's done the job far longer for far more people than any other. Remember the vile creature who baited God into torturing Job? We've often called him the Old Enemy, but—as we'll see—at times we seem to cherish him as much as despise him.

Three

THE DEVIL IN
DECLINE

*How did you come to fall from heaven, bright son of the
morning, how thrown to the earth, you who enslaved the
nations?*

—ISAIAH 14:12

*The devil's most clever trick is to convince us that he does
not exist.*

—CHARLES BAUDELAIRE

I think if the devil doesn't exist, but man has created him,
he has created him in his own image and likeness.

—FYODOR DOSTOEVSKY

Apollyon. Azazel. Beelzebub. Behemoth. Belial. The Evil One. Lucifer. Mastema. Mephistopheles. The Old Enemy. The Prince of Darkness. Sammael.

Satan.

Talk about somebody who needs no introduction. Millions of people around the world already have their answer, neat and complete, to evil—the existence of evil, the Problem of Evil. Under any of his many names, Satan is history's most widely feared and enduring cosmic villain.

If the world's evil and suffering *are* masterminded by a single supernatural entity, the Prince of Darkness has to be the prime suspect. True, the Devil's influence has waned considerably since, say, the 1500s, when the Europe of Columbus's time—and of the Spanish Inquisition—swarmed with witches, demons, incubi, succubi, and other vile agents of the Evil One. Yet he is only weakened, not gone. Satan remains a fearsome figure today for Jews, Christians, Muslims—and especially Floridians. On Halloween, 2001, the mayor of a little Gulf Coast town officially banned Beelzebub from the city: "Be it known from this day forward that Satan, ruler of darkness, giver of evil, destroyer of what is good and just, is not now, nor ever again will be, a part of this town of Inglis," proclaimed May. Carolyn Risher. Asked if she'd actually seen Satan in town, Risher replied, "Never. But I have felt his works."

If overzealous, Risher's far from alone. Today—at the dawn of the third millennium—some polls report that as many as 70 percent of Americans still believe in Lucifer. That figure underestimates the Devil's continuing hold over our secular, scientific, ironic age. For one thing, he long ago became deeply embedded in Western culture, and lives on in our myths, expressions, movies, TV shows, songs, and literature: The trajectory from Genesis to Goethe's *Faust* to *The Exorcist* is surprisingly direct. The enormous popularity of the Left Behind series of novels, based upon the New Testament's Book of Revelation, is further testimony to Satan's enduring place in our consciousness.

For another thing, even the most skeptical among us can appreciate the benefits of having a chief suspect, a one-stop culprit for all that troubles our lives, a Mr. Big to blame for the evil that so openly festers around us. But if Lucifer has long been our most popular explanation for the existence of evil, even he does not escape unscathed from closer scrutiny. True, his attractions are undeniable: terrific references, a long and impressive work history, and a killer attitude. But before we fix on Old Hairy as our final answer, we'd best check out his negatives—or would that be positives? We might find that Satan's personal bio is neither especially grand nor especially scary. Actually, it's a bit of a letdown.

To start with, our Prince of Darkness seems to have copied many of his fearsome traits and ugly tricks from older cosmic villains. Long before Satan, the Egyptians had Seth, who was associated with the color red. The Greeks had Pan (whence our word *panic*), a god of nature and fertility who had the horns, legs, and cloven hooves of a goat, and a sexual appetite to match. But these supernatural evildoers were neither all-powerful nor even all-bad. Like the humans who worshipped them, most had their good days and their bad days. As we've seen, scholars usually cite Angra Mainyu, preached in the seventh century B.C.E. by Zoroaster in what is now Iran, as the first 100 percent evil demon. Angra Mainyu was a key ancestor of Satan because his absolute badness meant that the good god (Zoroaster called him Spenta Mainyu) could be 100 percent good. Satan, as we shall see, later performed this same vital service for the Jewish/Christian/Muslim God.

So when does Satan arrive on the scene? Much later, and rather less grandly. Scholars say Satan started out as a figure in Hebrew tales around the sixth century B.C.E., but among Jews of that time he never quite ascended to the exalted position of Prince of Darkness and boss of all evil, as he did later in Christianity. The Hebrew word *satan* comes from a root word meaning "oppose" or "accuse." It was translated into Greek as *diabolos,* or "adversary," and then into Latin as *diabolus* and into English as *devil.* Anyway, "satan" was hardly on everybody's lips back in the pre-Christian Middle East; the word only appears a handful of times in the entire Old Testament, and never refers to the head of an "evil empire."

When Satan does show up in the Old Testament, he is a powerful supernatural being who disrupts human life, but only at God's command. In fact, there wasn't only one Satan, but numerous satans periodically sent by God to test or tempt humans. These were not lowly, despicable beings; they were angels, messengers of God, members of His royal court. In the story of Balaam and his donkey in the Book of Numbers, Yahweh sends a satan to block Balaam's path and to keep him from doing wrong. "I came here to oppose you," the satan says, speaking for Yahweh, "because your way is evil in my eyes."

Scholars say Satan gradually evolved into a quasi-independent source of evil as Judaism focused on one all-powerful, all-good God; here again pops up that pesky Problem of Evil: if God is all-good, where does evil come from? The Israelites' answer: Satan. But he had to be groomed for such a major role. One often-cited glimpse of Satan's rising star in Judaism is a comparision of two different Old Testament accounts of the same event, written several centuries apart.

The event was King David's unpopular step of ordering a census of Israel in preparation for taxation. In the earlier Book of Samuel, we're told this was God's idea: "The anger of Yahweh once again blazed out against the Israelites and he incited David against them. 'Go,' he said, 'take a census of Israel and Judah.'" Several centuries later, the Book of Chronicles records the same event this way: "Satan rose up against Israel and incited David to take a census of the Israelites."

Which was it? Is it possible that even Yahweh prefers to duck the blame for raising taxes? In any case, Satan is still not the full-fledged Prince of Darkness. In the Book of Job, as we saw, Satan destroys Job's wealth, murders his children, and covers him with boils to test his faith. But he does all this only with God's permission.

As Judaism evolved during the turbulent centuries before Christ, Satan gradually emerged as a better-defined and more powerful personality. So where is he supposed to come from? Most Christians probably remember Satan, or Lucifer (this name, Latin for "light-bearer," became associated with the morning star in the Isaiah passage on page *44*), as an angel driven from heaven by God after refusing to submit to His authority. This is the tale that became accepted Christian doctrine, but it wasn't the only one widely circulated. In fact, the Bible itself is packed with varied and sometimes contradictory accounts of Satan's emergence. Historian Jeffrey

Burton Russell reports that different passages in Scripture offer different views of Satan's fall: it was an ejection from heaven, or a voluntary departure; Satan fell from heaven to earth, or from heaven to the underworld, or from earth to the underworld; the fall happened before Adam's fall because Satan envied him, or about the time of Noah, or at Christ's birth, or at Christ's crucifixion; it will happen at the Second Coming, or one thousand years after the Second Coming.

And that's just the Bible! In the centuries just before and after Christ, a number of other stories were also widely written and read, including the odd tale that Satan was one of the so-called watcher angels banished from heaven for lusting after human women. This account was contained in Jewish writings that never made it into the Bible, but it is referred to in Genesis 6:1: "The sons of God, looking at the daughters of men, saw they were pleasing, so they married as many as they chose. . . . The sons of God resorted to the daughters of man, and had children by them." Then there was the early Christian Gnostic sect, which believed Yahweh was Satan.

Confused? Get in line. The rise of Christianity further cemented Satan's role as *the* Devil, the embodiment of evil and leader of the forces of darkness. Scholars cite the conflict between Jesus and Satan as the central theme of the New Testament, which shows the world split sharply between the forces of good and evil. Casting out demons, remember, was one of Jesus' signature accomplishments.

Historians say another, more mundane sort of conflict also contributed greatly to Satan's development: the fight between traditional Jews and the breakaway sect of early Christians. Though persecuted on all sides by pagans, both groups also struggled mightily against each other, accusing the other of causing disunity and preaching untruths. The ultimate culprit blamed for the other side's misdeeds? Satan.

Historian Elaine Pagels says the earliest stories of Satan agree "that this greatest and most dangerous enemy did not originate, as one might expect, as an outsider, an alien, or a stranger. Satan is not the distant enemy but the intimate enemy—one's trusted colleague, close associate, brother."

Satan continued to grow in power and importance as the Christian Church organized itself—it achieved official recognition under the Roman emperor Constantine in the fourth century. Outside official theological circles, the Evil One also evolved in myth and folklore, often blending in with other assorted malevolent demons, monsters, ghost, and giants. Satan was identified with animals, usually the snake, dragon, or goat. He could take on a variety of human forms and disguises, including that of a cleric or learned intellectual. Sometimes he was portrayed as lame because of his fall from heaven; his knees worked backwards; he had a second face on his stomach or rear end; he had horns, a tail, and cloven hooves; he was covered with black hair and had wings and an oversized phallus. Nor was the Devil always fearsome or invincible. The Middle Ages contributed their share of tales about stupid or defeated devils, including the story of how the English abbot Dunstan, suddenly confronted by the Devil, grabbed a pair of tongs from the fire and seized him by the nose. Howling in pain, the Prince of Darkness ran off and never returned.

But Satan hit his stride in the early Middle Ages, when it seems he was blamed for everything. It is probably impossible for most twenty-first-century Americans to grasp how palpably present Satan was in everyday life back then. Historian Paul Carus describes a thirteenth-century book written by one Abbot Richalmus about his constant confrontations with demons:

> *It is devils that make him feel qualmish when he has eaten too much; they make him fall asleep over his breviary. When he exposes his hand, they make it feel chilly; when he hides it under his cloak, they tickle and bite it like fleas. "Once," [the abbot] says, "when we were gathering stones for building a wall, I heard a devil exclaim, 'What tiresome work!' He only did it to tempt us and make us rebellious."*

Women were impregnated by the devil's nocturnal visits, and, of course, foolishly ambitious people made deals with the Devil, granting him their soul in exchange for worldy wealth and pleasure. The moral of such stories—at least from the perspective of the Church—was that people who displayed too much pride or ambition were mimicking Satan, whose pride and ambition got him tossed from heaven. And those who thirsted too much for knowledge of the natural world—which today we call science—were acting too much like Adam and Eve eyeing the Tree of Knowledge.

But even here, Satan was not totally without redeeming qualities. As Carus notes, while the human signatory to diabolical contracts might try to weasel out of the bargain at the end—sometimes with heaven's help—Satan always seemed to honor his side of the contract. "Although he is said to be a liar from the beginning, not one case is known in all devil-lore in which the Devil attempts to cheat his stipulators," Carus said. "Thus he appears as the most unfairly maligned person, and as a martyr of simple-minded honesty."

Satan really came into his own during the wars, plagues, and famines of the Middle Ages, and during the witch craze of the 1500s and 1600s, the Church-sponsored persecutions seeking to root out heresy, and the religious wars of the Reformation. The Devil's role was reenergized by the stern teachings of Martin Luther, who himself struggled constantly with Satan—once famously hurling an inkstand at him—and who identified the pope as the Devil on earth and regarded the Roman Catholic Church as a satanic bureaucracy.

Our modern picture of the devil comes primarily from the seventeenth-century epic poem *Paradise Lost*, by Englishman John Milton. Milton's Satan is a famously complex character: evil and hateful, to be sure, yet also glorious in a corrupted way (once an angel, always an angel), and almost dignified in his refusal to submit to God's authority.

> *He above the rest,*
> *In shape and gesture proudly eminent,*
> *Stood like a tow'r.*

The now-famous beginning of the tale has Satan, an angel in God's heavenly court, rebelling against heaven after refusing to bow down to God. The result is what you'd expect from taking on the Supreme Being.

> *Him the Almighty Power*
> *Hurled headlong flaming from the ethereal sky,*
> *With hideous ruin and combustion, down*
> *To bottomless perdition, there to dwell*
> *In adamantine chains and penal fire.*

Milton's Satan despairs at the loss of his former blissful existence with God, yet at the same time refuses to retract his prideful ways and seems intent on making the best of things, establishing his own wretched kingdom, with its capital, Pandemonium.

To reign is worth ambition, though in Hell:
Better to reign in Hell than serve in Heav'n!

Milton, a staunch Protestant, surely did not favor Satan over God. But many scholars have noted that the Evil One does seem to steal the show in *Paradise Lost*, emerging—at least to modern readers—as the most compelling and even the most sympathetic character. This portrayal of Satan as a defeated, yet defiant, rebel soldiering on against impossible odds was later championed by nineteenth-century Romantics such as William Blake, Lord Byron, and Percy Bysshe Shelley, themselves in rebellion against the entrenched religious and political order. A further bridge linking these notions to our age was provided by Shelley's wife, Mary, whose 1818 novel *Frankenstein* depicted a man-made "demon" who was innocent until corrupted by the world.

But by the eighteenth century, the increasing impact of science and rationalism on European minds had weakened Satan's hold on the popular imagination. The last great literary portrayal of Satan, Mephistopheles in *Faust*, by Johann Wolfgang von Goethe, presented a hornless, hoofless Devil who was as thoroughly modern as, say, a machine gun.

The Faust legend is based on a medieval story that

was one of the most popular tales in Christendom. It was revived in the sixteenth-century play *Doctor Faustus*, by Christopher Marlowe. Faust, or Faustus, is a learned, successful scholar whose thirst for even more wisdom leads him to flirt with the occult. The Devil appears to him in the guise of the ironic, sophisticated Mephistopheles—quite different from the clownish devils of earlier times—and agrees to grant supernatural powers to Faust for a fixed number of years in exchange for his soul. The deal is struck, and Faust is plunged into a world of unparalleled intellectualism and sensuality. At the end of his life, he realizes the enormity of his folly; in *Doctor Faustus*, he is dragged off to hell, but in *Faust* he is saved by the Virgin Mary.

Since the early nineteenth century, Satan's popularity has continued to decline, due to the combined effects of Darwinism, Marxism, and Freudianism, and also on account of biblical scholarship that challenged a wide range of accepted doctrines. How far the twentieth century distanced itself from the seventeenth is made clear by Freud's explanation of Milton's majestic and terrifying Satan; he regarded him as merely a psychological construct fueled by a child's repressed fantasies about being seduced by his or her father. Fire and brimstone evoked fearful visions in, say, the sixteenth century. But how can they compare to the vast, cold, mechanized savagery of the twentieth—to say nothing of the bionic, digitalized horrors yet to come in the twenty-first? Maybe the arsenal of evil available to humans has become too horrible even for Satan.

Some people say the general decline of belief in the Devil is a good thing, because it reflects a decreased tendency for us to blame evil on others or on powers outside ourselves. "Us versus them," they would say, is a dead end. But millions continue to believe in Satan, or in Islam's Iblis, as a real supernatural entity and the chief agent of world evil. In 1999, the Roman Catholic Church reaffirmed this view in publishing a revised manual for exorcism — the first update since 1614. "The existence of the devil isn't an opinion, something to take or leave as you wish," a Vatican official said, adding that the Devil "fools men by persuading them that they do not need God and that they are self-sufficient." Some polls report that more than one in three Americans expect the world to end as predicted in the Book of Revelation. Thought to have been composed around the year 95, Revelation overflows with bizarre apocalyptic symbolism and grand visions of vast plagues and firestorms and of battles between the forces of good and evil at the end of time. Its popular appeal, then and now, is based upon the comfort and encouragement it lends to persecuted Christians by describing the blissful future reserved for those who remain faithful to Jesus, and the savage punishments awaiting their persecutors.

So, two thousand years after his rise to stardom in

the New Testament, Satan is still on stage. He may have slowed a step and lost a lot of fan base, but he's hardly ready to be banished like a vanquished Napoleon to some remote islet where he can hold court, host video conferences, and sell T-shirts. What accounts for this staying power? Why do we still obligingly shudder at this old vaudevillian, reduced as he's been to being portrayed by the likes of Eriq LaSalle in the alarmingly bad 2002 flick *Crazy As Hell*. ("You've got to admit I'm great at the box office. At least, I hope I still am.")

He still is—and the likely reason is not because he's scary, but because he no longer is. Satan—today about as fearsome as Bluto—has become a familiar, even comfortable way of explaining away life's most discomfiting questions. As reflected in the old Latin saying *"Sine Diablo nullus Dominus,"* ("Without the Devil, there is no God"), the Evil One's chief role has always been to maintain cosmic balance. In lamenting that he is forbidden to worship God, Dostoevsky's Satan says: "[If I were to praise God,] the indispensable minus would disappear at once, and good sense would reign supreme throughout the whole world. And that, of course, would mean the end of everything."

Like Angra Mainyu before him, Satan is absolutely bad so that the Jewish and Christian and Muslim God can be absolutely good. But this is also why the Devil ultimately falters as Lord of Evil: in the end, he's just another being created by an all-powerful deity, another child of God performing according to the cosmic script written for all of us. And he's fighting a battle that — however grand and savage — we all know he's going to lose. Dostoevsky's Satan further complains, "Somebody takes all the credit of what's good for Himself, and nothing but nastiness is left for me."

It might be foolish to proclaim that Satan — along with God — is dead. But if we're determined to let God off the hook for evil, it might not be asking too much to wish for a more credible figure to shoulder the blame.

But wait — must we have a cosmic villain-in-chief? Modern evolutionary scientists say otherwise, and argue that it's time to stop fooling around with tacky Halloween characters cavorting in horns and hoofs. A clear-eyed, grown-up look at evil, they say, yields a perfectly satisfactory explanation that has nothing to do with Satan — or with God.

Four

SURVIVAL OF THE WORST

The devil under form of Baboon is our grandfather.

—CHARLES DARWIN

The principal and indeed the only thing that is wrong with the world is man.

—CARL JUNG

The human mind evolved to believe in gods. It did not evolve to believe in biology.

—EDWARD O. WILSON

"Evil," sniffs the *Oxford English Dictionary*, is "little used in modern colloquial English." Despite its renewed appearance in this Age of Terrorism, the word is medieval, striking an odd, overwrought note more suited to Stephen King or *Buffy the Vampire Slayer* than to the working vocabulary of the third millennium. This, of course, is largely the work of science. Churchgoing people and presidential speechwriters may lament it, but most of us no longer believe that the sun is borne across the sky in a celestial chariot, that crazy people are possessed by demons, or that illness is payback from an offended Deity.

So why, some scientists demand, do we insist on believing in some mumbo-jumbo mystery behind what we call "evil"?

Well, because we do. We still cling to the notion of morality as one of our "highest" human attributes. Even most post-Freudian, postmodern twenty-first-century sophisticates glow, however dimly, with fond belief that our sense of right and wrong arises from something grander than mere superstition, childhood trauma, or social conditioning. After all, we aren't just animals, right?

Wrong. Science tells us we are merely beasts, wallowing in our own instincts, whipsawed by the shifting pulls of our blind biological drives. What could "evil" mean then? What would happen to the elaborate ethical frameworks we've crafted, debated, lived by, and died for since long before Socrates chose hemlock? What about all those religious tax exemptions? How will William Bennett find work?

Good questions all. Because it happens that there's a nifty scientific explanation for the world's undeniable wickedness, one that knocks the stilts out from under our whole cast of scary supernatural characters, from Yahweh to Lestat.

In this view, the origin of evil comes down to two words: natural selection.

That's right: Charles Darwin, our favorite Victorian gentleman revolutionary, is back—to tell us that evil is a concept whose time is past. Traditional evil's most lethal adversary, it turns out, is not the rite of exorcism, or a crowd of peasants with pitchforks, or a hot babe who knows karate. It's evolutionary psychology, a relatively new area of scientific inquiry that applies Darwinism to the study of the origin and development of human behavior. If you accept the tenets of evolutionary psychology—or EP, as it's known to practitioners— you'll seek an understanding of evil by studying biology, not religion, metaphysics, astrology, or the *X-Files*. You will look at how other animals—especially chimps and our other close primate cousins—perform survival tasks like self-defense, mating, parenting, obtaining food, dealing with strangers, and so on. This can be unpleasant. Nature in the raw is no walk in the park. Ernest Becker wrote: "Life on this planet is a gory spectacle,

a science-fiction nightmare in which digestive tracts fit-
ted with teeth at one end are tearing away at whatever
flesh they can reach."

Most people today are at least somewhat resigned to
this *Texas Chainsaw Massacre* view of existence "in the
wild," even they we don't relish being reminded of it.
We've all heard of Darwin's 1859 *Origin of Species,* and
most of us accept some version of "survival of the fittest"
as the engine shaping how we and other living creatures
have evolved into our present forms. Why else did our
ancestors gradually develop an upright posture, binocu-
lar vision, opposable thumbs? The theory of evolution
through natural selection tells us that every new generation of humans contains genetic changes that arise in individuals by chance; the changes that are "selected" and
passed down to future generations are those changes — in
shape, color, speed, whatever — that help us succeed in
life's two grand projects: survival and reproduction.

Survival and reproduction. That's it. That's what all
life, including human life, is all about. Evolutionary
psychologists take this accepted biological theory and
apply it to the "higher" forms of human behavior, which
most social scientists see as arising chiefly from culture
rather than biology. But wait, EPs say: if natural selection drives changes in obvious physical features such as
height, hairiness, and body structure, shouldn't it also
shape the evolution of humans' brains and thus their
behavior? EPs say that it does, big-time — that our

brain is a "wet computer" and that, shaped by natural selection, it has over the centuries developed highly specialized circuits to support such "natural" activities as recognizing beauty, returning a favor, and sensing an enemy. "According to evolutionary psychology, neural tissue is no different from any other tissue," writes Edward Hagen of Berlin's Institute for Theoretical Biology. "It is functionally organized to serve survival and reproduction." This means that our most elemental sense of how to behave and the texts that express it—our Ten Commandments, our Golden Rule, our Gospels and sutras, our Boy Scout Oath—must also flow not from on high but from down below; in other words, from instincts shaped by the blind, pitiless struggle for survival. Humans' revered moral codes, the distinguished biologist Edward O. Wilson contends, "are very unlikely to be ethereal messages awaiting revelation, or independent truths vibrating in a nonmaterial dimension of the mind. They are more likely to be products of the brain and the culture."

If accurate, this means that the force that drives us to commit what we call "evil" is not the work of some bad-tempered supernatural entity; it's not a flare-up of our Jungian Shadow side or the result of psychological damage done by an overpunitive parent. None of that. It's simply the by-product of each individual's innate urge to survive long enough to pass his or her genes on to the next generation. "Evil," in other words, arises merely from a sort of neurological misfire rooted in the mechanics of our biological past—the occasional grunt that breaks through our elegant human oratory. Better yet, as Robert Wright put it in *The Moral Animal,* it's "the ghost of natural selection."

Say good-bye, Beelzebub.

So why do we humans routinely do evil things? EP says evolution moves so slowly that it takes tens of thousands of years or more for "selected" genetic changes to arise and spread through a population. If it's a terrific survival advantage to have longer, sharper canine teeth, for example, we wouldn't start seeing a lot of fanged people for something like fifty millennia. That means natural selection, like an outdated military strategy, has equipped us to fight the last war; our brain functions, like our physical ones, are adapted to conditions of the past. We modern humans, in other words, are wonderfully attuned to cope with the threats and opportunities presented by life wandering the Stone Age African savanna.

Remember, we emerged as skinny little creatures roaming naked across forests and grasslands. No fangs, no claws, no horns, no sharp hooves. Not even pepper spray. For more than 90 percent of our history, we lived in small, nomadic bands that spent their days gathering plants and hunting animals. "Each of our ancestors was, in effect, on a camping trip that lasted an entire lifetime," one evolutionary psychologist writes, "and this way of life endured for most of the last 10 million years."

It was a big, raw, dangerous world back then, ruled by predators; but over the millennia humans survived and prospered because they were clever scavengers, hunters, and warriors, and because they kept reproducing. That is, they foraged, fought, and copulated with great success. Today they still do, as they're still *programmed* to. But obviously our world has changed. A lot. And, by evolutionary time, in the blink of an eye. As another evolutionary psychologist phrased it: "Our modern skulls house a stone age mind."

Hagen offers a cute example in noting that our fear of being bitten by spiders and snakes—a fear developed over the last two hundred thousand years—remains stronger today than the much more recent, and realistic, fear of being hit by a car.

"Because two hundred thousand years is long enough for humans to evolve protective mechanisms but a hundred years isn't, we can predict that humans may well possess an innate aversion to spiders and snakes, but not to automobiles—even though far more people are currently killed by cars than by spiders or snakes."

Behold the biological origin of human wrongdoing: bred for the savanna, we've ended up in the suburbs.

Our journey from savanna to suburb began around ten thousand years ago, when human culture—ignited by the rise of agriculture, the explosion of population, and the development of hierarchical social systems—took off like a rocket. It has rushed ahead, relentlessly transforming itself, ever since.

But our brains and nervous systems, EPs say, are still stuck in the distant past. The result of this poor fit is crime and nasty acts generated by our ancient, bone-deep "evil" urges—today known as greed, aggression, and lust.

Take aggression. A few decades ago naturalist Konrad Lorenz raised eyebrows when he wrote that aggression was a natural instinct in the struggle for survival and reproductive success, which arguably makes aggression a long-term "positive" force. Among chimps and humans, this force is expressed as pride and status seeking, say Richard Wrangham and Dale Peterson in *Demonic Males:* "Pride obviously serves as a stimulus for much interpersonal aggression in humans, and we can hypothesize confidently that this emotion evolved during countless generations in which males who achieved high status were able to turn their social success into extra reproduction."

Surely *that* Stone Age attitude is still around. By the way, remember that pride also ranked worst among Christianity's Seven Deadly Sins and was the reason Lucifer fought God and fell from heaven.

As for group aggression, Wrangham and Peterson quote Darwin himself in explaining it as the natural flip side of group solidarity, which is another "successful" evolutionary adaptation. Darwin wrote: "A tribe including many members who . . . were always ready to aid one another, and to sacrifice themselves for the common good, would be victorious over most other tribes, and this would be natural selection."

It makes sense. Of course Stone Age humans would face dire physical confrontations with other humans or with animals; of course those humans bearing genes from the Vin Diesel gene pool would be more likely to prevail than those representing the David Spade gene pool. Sounds just right for the Stone Age.

But not for today; we've come too far, too fast. Humans have lost much of the original, concrete need for their aggressive instinct—fewer hungry tigers lurking on the way to the office, for example—without losing the instinct itself. Meanwhile, we've made astounding advances in the technology of assault. Our ability to accomplish aggressive projects has been multiplied a thousandfold, just as its traditional outlets have withered away and the planet has become ever more crowded. A tasty recipe for trouble.

Just imagine an African hunter-gatherer from a hundred thousand years ago—driving a huge, jacked-up Hummer (perhaps an elephant's thighbone in the gun rack)—trying to make it home early in rush-hour traffic. Road rage, anyone?

Such views helped plunge the precursor of evolutionary psychology, sociobiology, into a firestorm of controversy when they were first popularized in the 1970s by Edward O. Wilson and Richard Dawkins. Wilson argued that all social and moral behavior is primarily shaped by genetics and natural selection, not by God or by some sort of mystical "natural law." Dawkins proposed that humans are best viewed as "survival machines" guided by "selfish genes" rather than as, say, children of God put on earth to love Him and each other. Sociobiology drew howls of protest, and still does. Among its critics have been sociologists, theologians, and philosophers, all of them dubious about how much biology can be helpful on what's traditionally been their turf. Other critics slammed the discipline as racist and sexist (one college poster labels Wilson "the Prophet of Right Wing Patriarchy"), and they accused its practitioners of supporting a conservative political agenda that stresses deeply embedded genetic differences and downplays the possibility of changing human nature for the better. If human greed bubbles up from so deep in our core biological selves, critics asked, why bother trying to regulate freewheeling corporate capitalism? Or war? Opponents also linked sociobiology to eugenics, the early-twentieth-century pseudoscientific movement that sought to "improve humanity" by compulsory sterilization of those with "unfit" genes and by laws against interracial marriage, among other methods.

Wilson and other backers of sociobiology/EP heatedly deny such charges, but they linger. Part of the problem is the continuing legacy of social Darwinism, which was used as an excuse for permitting the rich and strong (individuals, corporations, nations, major league baseball teams) not only to dominate the weak but to prey upon them. A glance at the international corporate landscape today confirms that this ideology remains very much alive.

Even if all its critics are wrong, EP still provides a grim picture. Each of us is not only capable of so-called evil but is biologically programmed to commit it. What does this do to the grand debate? Are humans naturally good, as the eighteenth-century French philosopher Jean-Jacques Rousseau so famously proclaimed in his myth of the "noble savage" existing in a blissful, egalitarian "state of nature"? Or are humans born bad, corrupted from their first breath by the taint of original sin, as St. Augustine and many others have argued?

Neither, EP seems to say. Humans are born animals, struggling to do two things: survive and reproduce. Make that one thing: we survive in order to reproduce. In other words, it *is* all about sex.

Wilson, a distinguished scientist who's been hammered for years for his views, is still at it. In more recent writings, he's reaffirmed his belief that moral guidelines are simply biologically inspired "contrivances of the mind" favored consistently by a society long enough to be codified in a set of customs or laws.

Over time, Wilson says, these products—our moral

sentiments—become hardened into precepts, then into laws, and then, maybe, into "commands" said to be "received" from on high. In this process, he notes, these ethical codes typically solidified the power of ruling elites.

But why did such moral codes even arise? Wilson says religion is both an instinctual reaction to humans' need for meaning and for an escape from mortality, and a source of concrete survival benefits to members of "a powerful group united by devout belief and purpose."

Some will object to this facile (and here oversimplified) analysis as a dismissal of moral responsibility. They'll say EP is at best amoral, promoting selfishness, reducing criminals' blame, and undermining codes of right and wrong. And in a sense they'll be right. But even in an EP universe it would make practical sense to agree on basic rules of behavior so as to avoid chaos and crime. More broadly, most of us would likely agree that what makes most of us happy is "good," and what doesn't is "bad," and that we should join forces to ensure more of the former and less of the latter. This modest, mechanical approach—utilitarianism—may be all we have left in the way of a moral code. Not exactly Charlton Heston coming down from Sinai.

Other scientists think otherwise. They argue that humans, unlike other animals, are naturally moral because they have the mental power to anticipate the consequences of their actions, to make value judgments, and to choose between alternative courses of action. So, these scientists claim, humans' biological evolution *has* produced a unique inclination to choose between good and evil.

Wherever one ends up in this debate, evolutionary psychology poses a stiff challenge to traditional notions of evil. Wilson even says that "the choice between transcendentalism and empiricism will be the coming century's version of the struggle for men's souls." Maybe. But dwelling on that cosmic level, it's tempting to see EP as the apple in the Garden of Eden, the "knowledge of good and evil" that Yahweh forbade the first humans, the ultimate knowledge for which Faust sold his soul and that religions for centuries fought so bitterly to suppress—and it's no wonder they did.

But before you start scrambling up the Tree of Knowledge after that apple, note that the belief in natural selection as the source of "evil" is ultimately scarier than Satan. Old Hairy, at least, is a familiar foe who we know is going to lose in the end. And his very existence, however troublesome, testifies to the existence of a cosmic moral order that undergirds every soul, living or dead, and that promises an ultimate accounting. Satan, in other words, helps reassure us that yes, there *is* someone or something out there behind the sky.

Evolutionary psychology offers no such reassurance. Robert Wright wrote: "Sympathy, empathy, compassion, conscience, guilt, remorse, even the very sense of justice ... all these can now be viewed as vestiges of organic history on a particular planet."

That's cold. But even Wilson says EP is not necessarily incompatible with a belief in God or some other higher power—though one suspects the esteemed scientist is not exactly a regular on *The 700 Club*. For himself, Wilson says, "On religion, I lean toward deism [belief based on reason rather than revelation]." But he doesn't expect even the more popular varieties of religion to disappear anytime soon. "People," he writes, "will find a way to keep the ancestral spirits alive."

Of course we will. Evolutionary psychology may be a powerful tool for dissecting human behavior, and certainly it is a provocative one. (What about rape as a naturally selected male behavior?) But it still seems to fall short of explaining our most extreme eruptions of evil—our Idi Amins, say, or our Rasputins and Pol Pots. And for better or worse, few among even us denizens of the Digital Age seem ready to choose Darwin over Jesus, Moses, or Muhammad, not to mention Benny Hinn. Most Americans need a more emotionally fulfilling answer to the emotionally shattering challenge of evil, and they won't find it among the cool, rational tenets of EP—which, by the way, will also completely ruin the Halloween industry.

But before we rush out to rent *The Exorcist* again (why not just buy it?), let's consider another answer to evil offered by modern science. It's more fun than updated Darwinism. Then again, it's much more scary.

Five

POSTMODERN DEMONS

I wasn't some guy hanging out in bars, or a bum. . . . I was a normal person.

— TED BUNDY

The [psychopath's] reptilian, predatory eyes are, in a sense, the antithesis of the affectionate mirroring of the infant in the eyes of mother. The nascent self is reflected as an object of prey, rather than an object of love.

— DR. J. REID MELOY

*You don't understand me. You are not expected to. You are
not capable of it. I am beyond your experience. I am
beyond good and evil.*

— RICHARD RAMIREZ, THE "NIGHT STALKER"

*They wanted to know why I did what I did
Well sir I guess there's just a meanness in this world.*

— BRUCE SPRINGSTEEN, "NEBRASKA"

Science, as we've seen, has done its best to ruin evil, to strip it of all its poetry and mystery. No longer, except in front of glowing screens, do we cower before the demons and dragons, the giants, vampires, and sea serpents, that for centuries terrified our ancestors. We don't toss and turn at night, dreading the shameful visits of incubi or succubi. This seems to be a good thing. On the other hand, science hasn't abolished evil, as many once genuinely hoped it would. Instead, approaches like evolutionary psychology can only offer a sort of genealogy of evil that for most people fails to meet the immense challenge posed by wickedness — and that some critics charge even hints at justifying it.

But there's another line of contemporary scientific inquiry that lately has made great strides — or at least great books and movies — in addressing the more extreme cases of otherwise-inexplicable human evil. Unlike EP, it does feature a clearly defined villain, but this one bears no resemblance to Milton's snarling, splendidly ferocious Prince of Darkness. Instead, the villain is very much like Richard Djerf, a pale, chubby ex-grocery clerk in that most vanilla of towns, Phoenix, Arizona. No one ever suggested that Richard was a demon or a witch; indeed, a coworker at the market called him "a joy to work with." No one has quite been able to explain why he slowly, methodically butchered a family of four one warm afternoon a few years ago.

"I'm not crazy, I don't hear voices," Richard, then twenty-five and in jail, told a reporter in his soft, high voice. "I didn't have a terrible childhood. I just did what I did."

Behold modern society's leading candidate for evil incarnate: the psychopath.

"Intraspecies predators who use charm, manipulation, intimidation, and violence to control others and to satisfy their own selfish needs" is how pioneering Canadian psychologist Robert Hare described psychopaths, adding that "they cold-bloodedly take what they want and do as they please . . . without the slightest sense of guilt or regret."

Most of us—all fans of cop dramas—know something about psychopaths. Mention the word, and we immediately think of the fictional Hannibal Lecter, portrayed as educated, urbane, witty—a twenty-first-century version of Goethe's Mephistopheles. Or we recall all-too-real serial killers John Wayne Gacy, Ted

Bundy, Richard "the Night Stalker" Ramirez, and Albert de Salvo, also known as the Boston Strangler.

Actually, a better prototype of this popular nightmare was the lesser-known Eddie Gein, a Wisconsin farmer who lived alone on his crumbling family homestead until arrested for murder in 1957. Stunned police officers found a veritable treasure-house of horror at Gein's place, starting off with the headless body of a local woman hanging upside down from a meat hook and slit open down the front; her head and intestines were discovered in a box, and her heart on a plate in the dining room. Elsewhere officers came across the skins from ten human heads, the crown of a skull used as a soup bowl, a refrigerator full of human organs, the preserved skin from a female's torso, and other bizarre and repellent remains. Gein later admitted liking to wear the skin and other artifacts and pretending to be his dear, departed mother. If these grisly details sound familiar, that's because the Gein case at least partly inspired several popular films, including *Psycho*, *The Texas Chainsaw Massacre*, and, yes, *The Silence of the Lambs*.

Indeed, for Hollywood, psychopaths are hot. The word "psychopath" has become a staple on both the big and small screens; it is a label tossed around by prime-time homicide cops and assorted forensic specialists as loosely as judges and ministers tossed around "witch" in 1690s Salem, Massachusetts. Even in real life, the term seems to be often employed by law-enforcement officers, journalists, and politicians as an epithet meaning, simply, "a real bastard." A standard courthouse line is that most criminals pleading insanity are actually psychopaths: they're not "mad," in the sense of crazy, just "bad." It's worth noting, however, that most researchers consider true psychopathy to be a rare occurrence, turning up in 1 to 3 percent of the population, and overwhelmingly in men. Nor are most criminals psychopaths; Hare estimates, for example, that only about 20 percent of prison inmates are psychopaths. Still, these are busy people: Hare also believes psychopaths are responsible for more than 50 percent of serious crimes.

So what about our grocery clerk? Djerf was mad because he believed an ex-buddy had burglarized his apartment. So one afternoon Djerf tricked his way into his friend's family's house, tied up the mother and a younger brother, and waited for his ex-buddy to come home. As it turned out, the intended victim never showed. In the intervening hours, however, Djerf gradually and brutally killed both of his captives as well as his friend's father and teenage sister, who had the misfortune of coming home at their usual times. Djerf then doused the house with gasoline, turned on the stove, and drove off in the mother's car. Later, he reportedly told somebody the blood dripping from the mother's fatal wound was "really awesome."

The murder of vulnerable innocents is bad enough.

But especially chilling here is the *time* element: Richard did not kill in a convulsion of blinding rage or fear or lust; he did it over a period of hours—most of which were spent just . . . hanging out. Plenty of time to reflect upon exactly what he was doing. Plenty of time to stop. Why did Richard not stop? Clearly he was insane! Or not: a court psychiatrist found him "alert," "responsive," "free from obvious abnormalities in perception, memory or thinking," and "quite likely within the normal range of intelligence." He had no criminal record, no indications of brain damage, and no history of psychiatric illness, and apparently he had never abused drugs or alcohol. Richard's family life had been rather sad—his parents divorced, and he lived with his dad, who seemed neglectful. Sad—and possibly relevant—but far from horrible or even unusual.

So what are we left with? An ordinary young man from an unexceptional background who commits unspeakable atrocities for reasons no one, including him, can supply.

So much for science's triumph over religion. As philosopher Susan Neiman notes, modern examinations of evil have replaced blasphemy with pathology. But after dismissing the whole centuries-old cast of demons and ogres and Furies and the like, science leaves us with—nothing. This is an improvement over Satan?

Not that scientists haven't tried. The nineteenth-century French doctor Philippe Pinel used the phrase *manie sans delire* (insanity without delirium) for patients who behaved impulsively, destructively, and without remorse, but who nevertheless had normal reasoning ability. German psychiatrists later in the century coined the phrase *psychopathic inferiority*. In the early 1900s, the term *sociopath* was introduced by doctors who believed that conscienceless aggressive behavior was due primarily to poor socialization of infants and negative early childhood experiences. This competition among labels reflects one of the core disputes among researchers into psychopathy (or sociopathy): is it primarily a product of biology or of early childhood environment? That basic disagreement, so common throughout the social sciences, rages on today. And researchers face an additional problem—one that's always plagued rational appraisals of evil: psychopaths, like other humans who do evil things, tend to be cold, scheming bastards whom it is nearly impossible to observe neutrally. The result, in the words of forensic psychologist J. Reid Meloy, has been "generations [of researchers] that have contaminated scientific objectivity with moralizing."

Most researchers trace the modern view of the psychopath to Hervey Cleckley's 1941 book, *Mask of Sanity*. Cleckley identified psychopathic traits as guiltlessness, superficial charm, egocentricity, incapacity for love, absence of shame or remorse, lack of psychological

EVIL: A PRIMER

insight, and an inability to learn from past experience. Cleckley stressed that he was talking about something more than merely a hardened criminal:

> *The [psychopath] is unfamiliar with the primary facts or data of what might be called personal values and is altogether incapable of understanding such matters. . . . Beauty and ugliness, except in a very superficial sense, goodness, evil, love, horror, and humour have no actual meaning, no power to move him.*

Robert Hare devised a "psychopathy checklist" that's widely used in diagnoses. His litany of traits common to psychopaths includes glibness and superficial charm; a grandiose sense of self-worth; a strong need for stimulation; a pathological habit of lying; a manipulative nature; and a lack of empathy, remorse, or guilt.

A crucial point in all of this is science's nearly universal conclusion that psychopaths—despite the sick deeds they're capable of—are not sick. Not crazy. Not mentally ill. Not insane. This, despite the frustration of a judge quoted by Hare who, speaking of an offender whom psychiatrists pronounced sane but psychopathic, said: "Someone with such a history must be suffering from a mental illness, and if psychiatrists fail to realize [this fact,] they must be 'crazy' themselves." Actually, psychiatrists categorize crazy people as psychotic. The Diagnostic and Statistical Manual of Mental Disorders

(DSM), the official handbook of the American Psychiatric Association, defines psychosis as an illness that
involves "delusions or prominent hallucinations," and
that can include such symptoms as "disorganized speech
[and] grossly disorganized or catatonic behavior." The
most commonly diagnosed psychosis is schizophrenia.

The DSM does not directly define psychopathy.
Rather, most clinicians base that diagnosis on a DSM
category called Antisocial Personality Disorder (APD).
A personality disorder—there are several types—is not
a psychosis. It involves "an enduring pattern of inner
experience and behavior that deviates markedly from
the expectations of the individual's culture," and that is
manifested in ways like odd perceptions of the self and
others, inappropriate emotional responses, and poor
impulse control. People diagnosed with APD, in other
words, don't think they're Jesus or Napoleon and don't
receive secret coded messages from the CIA through
their TV sets. They are rational, alert, well situated in
reality; they know who and where they are and what
they're doing. But they do it anyway: they routinely pur-
sue their own selfish ends, take advantage of others, lie,
ignore the rules, act recklessly, abandon commitments—
all without caring about, or even thinking about, others'
fortunes or feelings. It's important to note, however, that
many or perhaps even most people with APD are not
what we'd call truly evil; many are not even criminals.
Some live among us as amoral political opportunists,

coldhearted business executives, professional gamblers, and small-time chiselers who are somehow able to talk their way through petty offenses, personal betrayals, bad debts, failed jobs, and ruined relationships.

Psychopaths, on the other hand, are not small-time. Meloy and other researchers believe that they do fit within the diagnosis of Antisocial Personality Disorder, but that they make up a small percentage of the APD population—those displaying aggression, self-centeredness, remorselessness, and other traits of the true predator. Some researchers consider psychopathy the explosive mixture of APD and another condition called Narcissistic Personality Disorder. This latter disorder, according to the DSM, involves "a pervasive pattern of grandiosity [in fantasy or behavior], need for admiration, and lack of empathy," resulting in individuals who are arrogant, envious, and exploitative. This conjures up an extremely powerful human drive: the search for the long-lost infantile pleasure of total gratification; the yearning to organize the universe, like a baby does naturally, totally around the needs and desires of numero uno.

So where do these modern demons come from?

Short answer: we don't know.

As noted, the debate continues between advocates of "nature" and advocates of "nurture," with most researchers taking a middle position. Advanced medical diagnostic techniques have detected abnormalities in the brains of psychopaths, leading some scientists to conclude that it's a "wiring" issue. But most remain wary of blaming neurological flaws for the whole range of antisocial behavior. Studies have found correlations between psychopathy and such factors as maternal deprivation during the first five years of life, child abuse and neglect, and brain injury. In 1989, James Dobson of the Christian group Focus on the Family conducted a famous eleventh-hour interview with Ted Bundy in which this killer of some two-dozen women blamed alcohol and pornography for his crimes. Most researchers seem to accept findings that psychopaths start young: they display marked antisocial behavior as children—technically called Conduct Disorder— including cruelty to animals, fire-setting, truancy, theft, and forced sexual encounters.

Or maybe psychopaths are best seen merely as "social cheaters," conditioned to be that way by natural selection. This provocative thesis is advanced by some advocates of evolutionary psychology including Ian Pitchford in *The Human Nature Review*. They suggest that it makes sense—in terms of evolutionary drives, that is— for socially disadvantaged males to employ deception, manipulation, and even violence to obtain resources and access to reproductive opportunities. As in the last chapter, we see how EP takes a second look at some of humans' so-called evil tendencies and pronounces them nasty, perhaps, but natural. "Given the paucity of evidence in favour of developmental instability and brain damage in psychopaths," Pitchford says, "the suggestion that psychopathy is an adaptation is worthy of further exploration."

As is the whole subject. Yet for our purposes the most stunning fact remains simply that psychopaths exist. That there *are* rational, intelligent humans among us who lack part of the emotional hardware that makes the rest of us "human." That our glorious human gifts of reason and perception and language can and do function equally well in the service of evil as in the service of good.

This, in turn, points towards some broader, and equally unsettling, conclusions: that humans are not basically good; that evildoing is as "natural" a state as goodness; that human practices of mutual respect and cooperation merely disguise a natural potential for savagery.

As our latest incarnation of evil, the problem of the psychopath exhausts all of our careful explanations, all of our rational campaigns. Ironically, for some it bolsters belief in what scientists would dismiss as superstition precisely because it defeats, or at least eludes, reason. The way is left open once again to believe in spirits. Is it that much more ridiculous—or less useful— to say that an aggressive, remorseless person is possessed or cursed than to label him a psychopath? Consider this passage from popular Christian evangelist Bob Larson's 1999 *Book of Spiritual Warfare:* "Narcissism is the soul of satanism. . . . Satanists feel no gladness in the pulse of life. The heartbeat of hell deadens their capacity to be touched by human compassion. . . . Power over their lives and the lives of others is all that matters." Substitute "psychopath" for "satanist" and delete the reference to hell, and the passage would fit fine in a psychiatric lecture. Like earlier standard-bearers of evil, the psychopath fascinates as well as repels us. Why are we so intrigued by Hannibal Lecter and his fellow monsters?

Romanticizing the psychopath is understandable. We each have our dark desires—a point forensic psychiatrist Robert Simon felt so strongly about that he entitled his book *Bad Men Do What Good Men Dream.* We naturally look with envy upon those few who commit the tabooed deeds that we secretly dream of committing, who break the rules, boldly tossing off the burden of morality and striking out towards a sort of absolute, outlaw freedom.

Is not this guiltless, totally self-centered world one vision of paradise?

But for all of his aggression and bravado, his self-confidence and charm, the psychopath seems almost universally experienced by clinicians and researchers as hollow to the core. The ultimate experience of the psychopath is one of a lack, of something missing. One thing that's clearly missing, of course, is a conscience, the sense of empathy with others that most of us take for granted. Curious how this "absence of good" echoes the ancient doctrines of Plotinus and of Augustine and other early Christian teachers who sought to explain how evil could exist in God's good universe. But psychopaths are missing more than just a sense of morality. Those who interact with them commonly report that there truly seems to be no *there* there—no internal life at all.

"Psychopaths experience chronic feelings of emptiness and of personal isolation," Simon writes. "They have . . . a need for constant stimulation, perhaps to dispel their diffuse sense of the meaninglessness of life." Deep within themselves, Meloy writes, psychopaths know "a profound, disquieting boredom."

At the end of the trail of the psychopath, evil's fiercest modern champion, we find . . . nothing. This is not encouraging. Nor does it immediately help our efforts towards a better understanding of evil.

Asked if he was sorry about butchering that innocent Arizona family, Richard Djerf—now on Arizona's Death Row—said he was. He admitted that slowly, methodically murdering two adults and two children was not his only choice that day: "I could have gone to a movie." The bleak moral landscape glimpsed in that remark is more chilling than any cemetery at midnight.

Six

THE MONSTER WITHIN

In every man, of course, a demon lies hidden.

—FYODOR DOSTOEVSKY

Evil is unspectacular and always human,
And shares our bed and eats at our own table.

—W. H. AUDEN

Indifference, to me, is the epitome of evil.

—ELIE WIESEL

Adolf Eichmann was, by all accounts, a remarkably ordinary man. He was born into a solid middle-class family, but did poorly in school and needed help from relatives to get a job. He was presentable, but not overly bright. Ambitious but often frustrated. By the late 1920s, he was a traveling salesman for an oil company. A good employee and law-abiding citizen, perhaps, but essentially a face in the crowd.

The particular crowd Eichmann joined, in 1932 at age twenty-six, was the Nationalsozialistische Deutsche Arbeiterpartei, or Nazi party. It turned out to be a perfect fit. Seven years later, through a combination of luck, hard work, and relentless careerism, he had risen to head Section IV B4 of the newly created Reich Main Security Office.

Eichmann's mission: the liquidation of the Jews in German territory. The Jewish Question.

The Holocaust, most would agree, was the most horrifying eruption of evil in the twentieth century—a century that offered plenty of competition. At the center of this unprecedented savagery hummed the Germans' vast bureaucratic machine of death, the ultimate demonic perversion of humankind's wonderful advances in science, technology, and industry. At the controls sat SS officers dedicated to carrying out Adolf Hitler's Final Solution—the methodical extermination of an entire race of fellow humans.

Near the very top of this hierarchy of evil sat

Obersturmbannfuhrer Eichmann, in charge of the roundup and transport of millions of men, women, and children from all over Europe to torture and death. This was no clock-watching bureaucrat, mindlessly feeding the interoffice mail. Though he protested after the war, "I never killed a Jew," Eichmann was fanatically devoted to his work, visiting Jewish ghettos and execution sites, pondering different schemes for the the Final Solution, taking on ever-increasing culpability for one of the most vile acts in human history.

How did he feel about his work? Eichmann told underlings: "I will jump into my grave laughing, because the fact that I have the deaths of five million Jews on my conscience gives me extraordinary satisfaction."

It's hard to conceive of a person more thoroughly imbued with evil, of a human being more in the thrall of the demonic. Surely Eichmann qualifies as a prime agent of whatever dark forces delight in human misery, his very existence silencing those learned rationalists who would dismiss the existence of evil forces on earth. Surely here is an authentic monster, whose life can help direct us to the foul origins of human wickedness.

If only it were that easy.

For at the center of the enigma that was Adolf Eichmann, we again find no firm answer to our quest for the origins of evil. The core is hollow. Despite the unimaginable horrors he visited upon humankind, Eichmann to the end remained nobody special, a garden-variety human being, a face in the crowd. And this radical conclusion comes not from some neo-Nazi "revisionist" historian, but from a celebrated twentieth-century political philosopher who was herself a refugee from the Nazis.

In 1960, Hannah Arendt attended the war-crimes trial of Eichmann in Jerusalem, where he'd been brought by Israeli agents who'd kidnapped him from his postwar hideout in South America. To her profound surprise Arendt, herself a Jew, beheld a man "quite ordinary, commonplace, and neither demonic nor monstrous." Her startling conclusion: massive, horrifying evil could erupt from bland, nondescript men and women who lack even "firm ideological convictions or . . . specific evil motives."

Arendt put forth this proposition in the subtitle of her book on the trial: *A Report on the Banality of Evil*. In doing so she coined a phrase that still stirs controversy four decades later. In a later work, Arendt, who died in 1975, wrote: "I held no thesis or doctrine [when coining the phrase], although I was dimly aware of the fact that it went counter to our tradition of thought—literary, theological, or philosophic—about the phenomenon of evil."

Evil people, she noted, are supposed to act out of pride, envy, weakness, hatred, or greed. "What I was confronted with was utterly different and still undeniably factual. I was struck by a manifest shallowness in [Eichmann] that made it impossible to trace the incontestable evil of his deeds to any deeper level of roots or motives."

Instead of the spawn of Satan, Arendt encountered a calm, polite man who seemed incapable of speaking except in clichés, even when they contradicted his past utterances or were grotesquely inappropriate to his status as a man with the blood of literally millions on his hands. He seemed, as he repeatedly claimed, to have no particular hatred for Jews. He spoke at great length to his Israeli interrogators about his past frustration at not receiving promotions within the Nazi hierarchy. Examining psychiatrists pronounced him normal, with one calling his psychological outlook "not only normal but most desirable." A religious minister who regularly visited him in prison called Eichmann "a man with very positive ideas."

As psychiatrist Bernard Bergen noted, it was as if Eichmann was not just reluctant but somehow incapable of reflecting upon his ghastly past. In Jerusalem, "Eichmann had nothing new to say about himself 15 years after the horrendous crimes he had committed." Given the novel *Lolita* to pass the time in his Israeli jail, he indignantly returned it, telling his guard, "Quite an unwholesome book." Even Eichmann's last words on the gallows, uttered after he'd walked calmly from his cell and refused a hood, displayed what Arendt called a "grotesque silliness." Among other things, he said: "After a short while, gentlemen, we shall all meet again. Such is the fate of all men. Long live Germany, long live Argentina, long live Austria. I shall not forget them."

Huh? Eichmann was so deeply embedded in a world of clichés, Arendt wrote, it was as if "he forgot that this was his own funeral."

She then posed a question that still haunts the effort to understand evil: Can people commit evil acts without having evil motives? "Is wickedness . . . *not* a necessary condition for evil-doing?"

Arendt's book unleashed a storm of criticism from those who believed she was downplaying the unique horror of the Holocaust and the suffering of the Jews. How, they demanded, could such massive savagery be in any sense labeled "banal"?

The furor was magnified by the truly staggering effect that the Holocaust had—and continues to have—upon the efforts of Western thinkers to understand evil. As philosopher Susan Neiman notes in *Evil in Modern Thought*, many thinkers simply threw up their hands, concluding that Auschwitz and the other elements of the Holocaust introduced a level of wickedness that mocks any attempt to explain it. "What seemed devastated—nay, entirely thwarted—by Auschwitz was the possibility of intellectual response itself. Thought stood still, for the tools of civilization seemed as helpless in coping with the event as they were in preventing it." Arendt's defenders, such as Neiman—who calls *Eichmann in Jerusalem* "the twentieth century's most important philosophical contribution to the problem of evil"—say her point was that even the most extreme evil can arise among everyday humans, that the monstrous can become commonplace. That the work of genocide can became just another day at the office. That, given the right circumstances, each of us is capable of being Adolf Eichmann.

Another crucial element of Arendt's view, as she herself recognized, was that it abandons the generally accepted idea that evil acts must be intentional acts. "Foremost among the larger issues at stake in the Eichmann trial," she wrote, "was the assumption current in all modern legal systems that intent to do wrong is necessary for the commission of a crime." Somehow, that familiar and wholly reasonable assumption seems to break down in the face of evil perpetrated on such a vast and savage, yet "legal," scale. Perhaps one lesson here is that today's huge bureaucratic societies—in which hierarchy, standardization of procedure, and obedience are increasingly essential for ensuring the most mundane of daily needs, from commercial aviation to clean water supplies—can no longer permit the luxury of individual moral deliberation. As a result, "evil" could be increasingly considered what the latest poll or pundit or political star says it is; if enough of us accept a doctrine or policy, doesn't that make it the norm? Arendt wrote:

> *The trouble with Eichmann was precisely that so many were like him, and that the many were neither perverted nor sadistic, that they were, and still are, terribly and terrifyingly normal. This new type of criminal . . . commits his crimes under circumstances that make it well-nigh impossible for him to know or to feel that he is doing wrong.*

As Neiman writes, the consequences for our understanding of the world are enormous: "The problem of evil began by trying to penetrate God's intentions. Now it appears we cannot make sense of our own."

But how did we get to this point? Arendt didn't claim to have an answer. But she speculated that the very act of thinking might be among the conditions that make men refrain from evildoing, or actually condition them against it. In Eichmann, she claimed, "the only notable characteristic one could detect . . . was something entirely negative: it was not stupidity but *thoughtlessness.*"

Thoughtlessness. Maybe another word for taking the easy way out, for surrendering to the party line, settling for the conventional wisdom, the stereotypes and clichés and "expert commentary" that swirl ever more thickly about us. For fleeing doubt in pursuit of what one writer called "the delirium of blind loyalty."

Such blissful blindness! Listen to what exactly Eichmann lamented in recalling his sadness at Germany's defeat: "I sensed I would have to live a leaderless and difficult individual life, I would receive no directives from anybody, no orders and commands would any longer be issued to me, no pertinent ordinances would be there to consult—in brief, a life never known before lay before me."

Besides the stunning self-centeredness, note that Eichmann mourns the loss of his sealed, ordered little world in which he could lose himself and his individual moral identity. For him as for us, the burden of thinking weighs heavily; the moral demands thrust upon us as independent, rational individuals can seem too much to bear. Drenched in information, buffeted by competing ideologies, surrounded by experts, pummeled by nonstop commercial appeals, how tempting it is to let our minds shut down and simply join up—with some welcoming institution, bureaucracy, subculture, belief system. And if someday our own small role in that large and complex enterprise requires us to break a few formal moral rules, who exactly will be to blame? Good question, notes Andrew Delbanco: "Arendt's most frightening implication was that the concept of evil might actually be incompatible with the very nature of modern life."

Is this how extraordinary evil arises in ordinary people? Maybe, but even Arendt cautioned against taking

much solace in such a discovery: "It was a lesson, neither an explanation of the phenomenon nor a theory
about it."

A lesson taught by Adolf Eichmann, a remarkably
ordinary man.

Seven

HEINOUS, CRUEL, DEPRAVED

The gods were bored; therefore they created human beings.

—SOREN KIERKEGAARD

The unrighteous man . . . had far better not be encouraged in the illusion that his roguery is clever; for men glory in their shame.

—PLATO

Life and death should not be determined by such niceties of language.

—JUSTICE THURGOOD MARSHALL

Want a good scare? *Dracula,* the original 1897 novel by Bram Stoker, remains a truly frightening read. Alfred Hitchcock's *Psycho* terrified millions, as William Friedkin's *The Exorcist* did years later. Stephen King has been scaring delighted readers by the millions for years.

All this is fun. This is scary, but it's fun-scary. When we exit the multiplex, close the book, or switch off the TV, what we're really afraid of—whatever our spiritual persuasion—is that mundane form of evil called crime. This, it turns out, is wise. As we saw in the last chapter, everyday evil can metastasize into gigantic spectacles of horror that dwarf the scariest myth or Gothic tale. Still, the wickedness most likely to flash into our lives is that which festers through the daily deeds of the seemingly normal people around us—the guy in the next car, the family that lives two blocks over, the couple we met at the bar.

The shrine to this most ancient and pervasive of evils is no farther away than the local courthouse: "Victim was strangled by her own oxygen tubes, physically and sexually assaulted while alive or at the point of death." This horror wasn't the work of some caped nocturnal man-beast who feeds on human blood. Nor was Satan anywhere in sight when the: "[victim's] body [was] broken, crushed, torn, scraped, shot, dragged, beaten and bruised; shot three times."

Compared with the majestic poetry of, say, the

Book of Revelation, these neatly typewritten accounts are bone-dry: "The defendant killed four human beings without justification or excuse. The defendant's state of mind was illustrated by his comment, 'You should have seen Charley when I hit him with those cutters.'"

These snapshots of the human heart at its worst come from transcripts of an American criminal court, where identifying, classifying, and responding to human wickedness are business as usual. It is here that centuries of Western meditations on evil—codified in our criminal laws—are applied to concrete acts by real people. Where philosophy and theology hit the street. The legal approach, which seeks to be secular, universal, and just, is designed and constantly adjusted to reflect and reinforce our core social values. What better place to seek an understanding of evil? There's also an another good reason: metaphysics is nice, but legal conclusions can have an immediate and decidedly nontheoretical impact. If you violate Immanuel Kant's famous "categorial imperative," for example, it's not clear what will happen—even if you're among the few who actually understand Kant. But violate criminal law, and you could be modeling an orange jumpsuit.

True, the criminal justice system doesn't normally mull the deep origins of evil, except perhaps in the rare cases of insanity pleas. Cops, lawyers, judges, and legislators usually avoid the flamboyant language of religious fundamentalists or the mental acrobatics of early Christian theologians. But they're all talking about the same thing.

"Defendant retained victim's necklace and charm as a souvenir; defendant participated in a celebration of murder where group played song, 'We Are the Champions.'" Unspeakable acts such as these are far too common. However, the crimes described in the transcripts are not typical. They are capital offenses—those rare acts that America's thirty-eight death-penalty states consider so wicked that they merit the ultimate punishment. About thirty-seven-hundred prisoners sit today on Death Row in the United States, out of the nearly 2 million locked up in its prisons and jails. These Death Row inmates are, officially, the worst of the worst. They've been convicted of the most savage acts, the ones that are beyond forgiving, that cannot be redeemed. Acts that so brutally abuse our most precious values—and so threaten our fragile social consensus—that they must be harshly punished. In one important sense, the list of these acts defines the limit of evil our society will abide.

The list is short. Among the states with the death penalty, a few at least officially permit its use in cases of aircraft hijacking and for some sexual assaults, but most reserve it for certain kinds of premeditated murder—known variously among the states as "first-degree murder," "capital murder," "aggravated murder," and "intentional murder." How do we decide which convicted murderers should be executed? Death-penalty states today do so by consulting a list of so-called aggravating and mitigating factors that help juries decide just how severe the punishment should be. This practice grew out of a 1972 U.S. Supreme Court decision that said the death penalty is constitutional, but that the Eighth and Fourteenth Amendments forbid a judge or jury from imposing it arbitrarily. Choosing from lists of aggravating and mitigating factors has been accepted as the best way to prevent that.

Once a defendant is convicted of murder in a case in which the prosecutor seeks the death penalty, the court reconvenes in a sentencing hearing. Prosecutors offer aggravating factors to show that the defendant deserves to die. Defense attorneys offer mitigating factors to demonstrate the opposite. Jurors weigh both sides in concluding precisely how evil this particular murderer is.

A survey of aggravating factors contained in various state statutes quickly reveals several that are common to most or all. This is to be expected, as all states answer to the same Supreme Court. Here, then, are some of the deeds that we Americans have legally determined to be, as one law review article puts it, "the most egregious and reprehensible type of behavior in our society today."

Killing or "creating a great risk of death" to more than one person. The straight quantitative approach, especially relevant to a highly mobile society packed with semiautomatic firearms.

Killing by a defendant previously convicted of a serious violent crime. We are especially outraged at this behavior by someone who already escaped execution for antisocial violence, and we are increasingly certain that he or she would do it again.

Killing while committing rape, kidnapping, robbery, or another serious crime. This category, sometimes called "felony murder," has been assailed by critics who claim it muddies up the all-important question of intent. How, they asked, can a murder committed in the heat of a robbery be "premeditated"? Such objections were not persuasive.

Killing for hire. Even Deuteronomy warns, "A curse on him who accepts a bribe to take an innocent life." The hit man is commonly portrayed in fiction as a soulless vessel of pure evil—though, interestingly, often still an attractive one. Indeed, the professional killer may generate fear and disgust, but he also generates awe, presumably because he's brushed aside the somber moral strictures the rest of us meekly accept, stepped boldly across the line, and tasted of the forbidden freedom (kind of an apple taste?) known only to those who would dare play God. Or so we imagine. From *The Seven Samurai* to James Bond to Sammy "the Bull" Gravano, we have long tended to envy as well as revile paid killers, and we afford them special consideration in our execution rituals. On the other hand, ours is a society that increasingly reveres the no-nonsense commercial approach; everything is now said to proceed better if it's "run like a business." So why single out someone who is simply fulfilling a labor contract?

Killing an especially vulnerable victim. This could be a disabled or elderly person, an ill or injured one, a child or captive, or anyone who lacks the capacity to defend themselves. Here we as a society seek to extend extra protection (via deterrence) to the weakest among us, presumably prompted by the conviction that it's more evil to deliberately kill when the killer "doesn't have to," and that it's more evil to kill those easiest to kill. Of course, the wholesale slaughter of an enemy's elderly, women, and children has long been a feature of warfare, from the Old Testament to the American West. But that's not evil, we're told—that's just war.

Killing a police officer, a judge, a court witness, or a firefighter; killing while in jail or prison, or while escaping. Here the law's role in calibrating our scales of moral outrage is influenced by the practical need to keep those who staff the front lines of the system showing up for work. It may be smart social policy to threaten greater punishment for killing a police officer than for killing, say, a mailcarrier. But it's not immediately clear in what sense taking the life of the former is more wicked. True, police officers are entrusted with the difficult and even noble mission of keeping the peace; but doctors and teachers and social workers perform noble public functions too.

Killing an elected official or a candidate for office. No jokes, please.

Killing a child. This one registers immediately on the visceral scale. It's hard to imagine anyone who wouldn't recoil in horror at the prospect of deliberately murdering a child—despite the fact that this evil has been openly practiced in places like Rwanda, Bosnia, and the Middle East. And calling it "collateral damage" doesn't help. Children are our beloved, our better selves, our symbols of innocence and hope for the future. So American society proclaims it irredeemably evil to murder anyone under fourteen. Or under thirteen. Or twelve. Turns out that different states have established different ages at which the victim's murder becomes unspeakably evil, as opposed to just very, very bad.

Killing a hostage. This is a special case within the "vulnerable" category, and again the strict moral basis for adding it separately to the roster of horrors is not immediately apparent; why is killing a hostage worse than killing just any wheelchair-bound grandma? The answer likely is again a practical one—the goal of discouraging kidnappers and aiding police negotiators trying to defuse a "barricaded gunman" situation.

Killing from ambush. Anybody who's ever watched

a Western knows that the hero never hides behind those classic Arizona boulders in order to attack the villains. Such ambushes are effective, but cowardly, and thus apparently evil.

The fact that such stratagems were commonly used in the Old West doesn't seem to matter. It certainly could matter in the cases against John Allen Muhammad and John Lee Malvo, charged in the shooting of thirteen people from ambush—ten fatally—in the Washington, D.C., area in the fall of 2002. The widespread panic and social dislocation caused by this thirty-nine-day series of ambushes does seem to reinforce the appropriateness of this aggravator.

Killing in an especially heinous, cruel, or depraved manner. What? To the nonexpert, this item could sound distressingly vague, a sort of catchall category so open to interpretation as to be almost meaningless. Turns out many experts agree. This "aggravator," in fact, often abbreviated "HCD," has been criticized for years as imprecise and troublesome, repeatedly being questioned by scholars, defense attorneys, appeals courts, and the U.S. Supreme Court itself. In the case of similar language in Georgia law, for example, the high court once complained that it could "fairly characterize almost every murder as 'outrageously or wantonly vile, horrible and inhuman.'"

The *Oxford English Dictionary* says the word *heinous* comes from the French word meaning "to hate." It means "hateful . . . highly criminal or wicked." *Cruel* comes from the Latin for "morally rough," and means "showing indifference to or pleasure in another's distress." Cruel people are "disposed to inflict suffering [and to be] merciless; pitiless."

The word *depraved* comes from the Latin for "perverted" or "corrupted," which is based on a word for "crooked" or "wrong." It means "rendered morally bad." Interestingly—for we never stray far from our religious roots—the *OED* also notes that the phrase *total depravity* is commonly used to refer to "the innate corruption of human nature due to Original Sin."

For older Americans, the words *heinous, cruel,* and *depraved* were incarnated in the figure of Charles Manson, the career criminal who enticed his cult followers to commit several bloody murders in the summer of 1969. At the home of film director Roman Polanski, they shot and stabbed five people, including pregnant actress Sharon Tate, who pleaded for her baby's life. The next night they slaughtered a married couple and left slogans written on the walls in their blood. Even Anton LaVey, then newly famous as founder of the Church of Satan—and somebody who should know about evil—called Manson a "mad-dog killer" and said he deserved the death penalty.

A more recent high-profile example was the 1998 murder of Texan James Byrd Jr., an African-American man whom three white men chained by the ankles to the back of their truck and dragged for three miles, finally dumping the dismembered corpse in front of a Black church. *Hateful, pitiless, perverse, wicked*—the words seem specially created for that June night in Jasper, Texas.

While powerful, these words remain vague. As a result, some courts have tried to define them even further; Arizona law, for example, lists five factors that can be considered to determine if the defendant's state of mind was "especially heinous or depraved":

- The defendant apparently relished the murder. In one case, the murderer bragged about the killing, gave away bullets as souveniers, "and complained that the bullets should have made a larger hole."
- The defendant inflicted gratuitous violence, which basically means more than necessary to kill. In one case, for example, "Three stab wounds were fatal and thirty-seven others were excessive."
- The defendant mutilated the victim after death, "reflecting a mental state that is marked by debasement."
- The issue of senselessness is considered when the murder was unnecessary for the defendant to achieve his or her criminal goal, as in killing an infant before robbing her parents.
- The issue of the victim's helplessness arises when the victim is mentally or physically disabled and so unable to resist.

Is this clearer? Maybe, but it's also repetitive—the "helplessness" factor was already covered—and, yes, still pretty vague. In the absence of some sort of bragging, how easy is it to tell after the fact whether a killer "relished" his deed? Further, is it realistic to expect a killer to know, in the heat of the moment, just how much violence is "necessary"?

A more serious point of contention is the issue of mutilation. Surely most of us are disgusted and enraged by killers who sexually assault or cut up, burn, or otherwise mutilate their dead victims. Few would deny that this reflects a "depraved" mind, whatever that might exactly mean. But just how evil is any deed perpetrated upon a person who's already dead? It may sicken us, and it may be a separate crime to desecrate a corpse, but it surely doesn't cause further pain and suffering to the victim. Besides forcing courts to wrestle with such unpleasant questions as what constitutes mutilation, such issues have also prompted them to ask how close in time to the actual murder the mutilation occurred—a factor that could determine whether the killer was "depraved" at the time he or she actually killed, and not just afterwards. As a result, some state courts have ruled that the HCD factor can only apply to torture or severe physical abuse of the victim before death, and that whatever deranged specimens like Jeffrey Dahmer do after death is irrelevant.

A final note: The suffering caused a victim before

death can be mental as well as physical. The former would include "a victim's contemplation of his or her ultimate fate . . . and watching or hearing a loved one die while knowing the victim will be killed next."

So where does this official tour of depravity leave us? It reminds us that the "ordinary" evil of violent crime can easily be as terrifying as any visit from Count Dracula or Michael Myers, while also being a) much more common and b) real. It's hard to top, for example, the fear that gripped the Washington, D.C., area during the month of sniper killings—quite in the absence of any supernatural phenomena. It's hard to imagine greater horror and outrage than those caused by Timothy McVeigh's bombing of the Oklahoma City federal building. And McVeigh, an upstanding middle-class army veteran who went to his death unrepentant, fit nobody's image of a villain.

Our day in court also raises two further points. One is that we can't forget the role of pain, especially gratuitous pain, as an indispensable element of evil. In researching the "aggravators" and related legal doctrines, we repeatedly encounter torture as an act that separates the evil from the merely bad. Torture, we might note—the needless imposition of suffering—sounds like the act of somebody playing God. A second, related point is that of imbalance: murdering a vulnerable victim, a child, a hostage, even murdering from ambush, suggest a concept of evil linked to a radical imbalance between pepetrator and victim. The more power we have in a situation, that is, the more evil we are to abuse that power.

On the other hand, the incurable vagueness of the HCD factor once again confirms the difficulty—the futility?—of seeking an airtight definition of evil. Even in our temples of justice, reason must ultimately give way to gut feelings—in this case the gut feelings of twelve jurors. This might be inevitable—remember Justice Stewart's remark, "I know it when I see it"— but it clearly presents problems. For example, many people of a particular race, creed, or color may have a gut reaction against people not like them. This is no basis for justice.

And many of us dutifully cling to conventional defi- nitions of wrongdoing even when our rational minds tell us not to. Take the venial sin of cursing: most of us were taught that cursing is bad, and religions typically condemn it as at least flirting with evil. But a closer look suggests otherwise.

Eight

PIGS IN YOUR CEMETERIES

You shall be a fugitive and a wanderer over the earth.

—YAHWEH TO CAIN, GENESIS

May he who steals you then be sent
A blow upon his fundament.

—CURSE INSCRIBED IN A THIRTEENTH-CENTURY
BOOK TO WARD OFF THIEVES

It's morning rush-hour hell. You're late, you're groggy, you've spilled boiling hot coffee on your thigh, and you've just inched your way to the crest of the freeway ramp when some swine tries to cut in front!

"Goddamit!" you scream. "Wait your turn!"

"Go to hell!" he yells back with one raised finger.

Wait. Please. This all-too-common exchange is regrettable for two reasons. First, of course, it's vulgar and offensive. OK, but you're mad. Then there's the second, more serious drawback: it's boring.

Listen to yourselves. "Goddammit"? "Go to hell"? This is embarrassing. Maybe you'll get really creative and toss in the f-word.

Could this be why there's so much road rage — nobody knows how to curse anymore?

The *Anchor Bible Dictionary* defines cursing as "to predict, wish, pray for, or cause trouble or disaster on a person or thing," and most of us dutifully condemn it as a regrettable habit that in a better world would be limited to the drunk, the disreputable, and the surprised guests on *Jerry Springer* ("I just hope that *BLEEP! gets ahold of* your *BLEEP!* and *BLEEEEEEP!!*") Historically speaking, however, this dismissal does not fit. Instead, cursing turns out to be a tradition that dates from humans' earliest recorded speech and that has been engaged in by princes and prophets, gods and sinners, literary masters and illiterate peasants. Cursing, the most popular form of invoking evil, has been around forever and is here to stay.

So can we please pay some attention to style?

Imagine yourself back at that ramp. When the scoundrel makes his move, you roar, "May ravens tear your eyes out while you hang high on the gallows!" in your best Old Norse accent.

Or, you go Irish: "May pigs dig up your cemeteries!"

Or you brandish the Bible: "You will eat the fruit of your body, the flesh of those sons and daughters of yours whom Yahweh has given you!"

On the other hand, you could let the wretch off easy with an African wish: "May you marry your mother-in-law!"

Wouldn't any of these be better than monosyllabic grunts and vulgar gestures? And certainly an artful curse would be a vast improvement over a punch in the face or a nine-millimeter pistol slug.

True, cursing is not nice. Also true: it's only natural to occasionally wish evil upon others—indeed, sometimes they deserve it. Perhaps our more realistic goal should be to occasionally indulge in bad words—formally known as maledictions—while refraining from bad deeds. Even *The Catholic Encyclopedia* says that "imprecations that spring from impatience, little outbreaks of anger over petty annoyances, and those spoken . . . under impulse . . . are, as a rule, only venial sins." It's even permissible to call down evil "as a punishment for misdeeds," the *Encyclopedia* adds, and it's always fine to curse the Devil. And it's worth asking how bad it can be to invoke vengeance from gods and spirits that few of us believe in anymore. Today, even most Christians and other believers doubt they can really call down evil from above. We still might get the creeps watching Brendan Fraser in *The Mummy*, but who really expects, say, a swarm of those big, hideous bugs to show up at the door?

In fact, the case can be made that cursing has a positive role to play in human affairs:

- Cursing is an excellent way of venting anger.
- Curses reflect mankind's reverence for its most precious gift: language.
- Curses are quintessentially egalitarian, offering put-down power to any ordinary person, not just to the privileged and powerful.
- Cursing is at bottom a spiritual act, rooted as it is in belief in a supernatural power.
- Cursing could help the economy: if we could revive the ancient Mediterranean practice of employing professional scribes to compose high-quality, up-to-date curses, just consider the job-creating potential.

Think about it: if we chose a broad medley of different deities to invoke, the practice would be more fun—and even educational for the cursee. And think of the social kismet. Imagine being blasted in the grocery express lane by a complete stranger who calls upon the same pre-Christian Mesopotamian nocturnal female vampire that you do! It might still smart, but at least you'll be networking.

"The hand of the executioner shall drag you around, while the people applaud, and his hook shall be driven into your bones," wrote the Roman poet Ovid, apparently in a bad mood. "With talons and beak the merciless vulture shall pull out your guts, and voracious dogs shall tear apart your treacherous heart, and over your body shall rage fights of insatiable wolves."

Get the idea?

Curses have been used since ancient times to punish enemies and wrongdoers, to recover stolen property and guard secret rituals, to seek revenge and protect shrines, grave sites, and books from harm.

Historian S. A. B. Mercer wrote: "The malediction in Babylonian and Assyrian times was a highly developed legal and religious ceremony, universally practiced and respected." Or listen to Christopher Faraone and Dirk Obbink in *Magika Hiera:* "At some point in their lives virtually every man and woman would have had the option of recourse to these traditional rites to learn about the future, turn the head of a potential lover, or prevent plague and other diseases from falling on their families and flocks."

While we usually associate cursing with the spoken word, it wasn't all just hot air. One of its more intriguing historic forms was the "curse tablet," used for centuries throughout the Mediterranean world from the fifth century B.C.E. to the time of imperial Rome and after. These were thin sheets of lead on which a person inscribed a plea to various gods to defeat, hamper, control, injure, or kill an enemy. Often professional scribes did the work for a fee, and the tablets, commonly known by their Latin name, *defixiones*, were then deposited in a fresh grave, tossed in a river or down a well, or buried in a graveyard—all to get them closer to the underworld gods whose help was usually being sought.

"Burial sites of those who had died young or by violent means were the preferred choices," writes John Gager in *Curse Tablets and Binding Spells from the Ancient World*, "because it was believed that their souls remained in a restless condition near the graves until their normal life span had been reached."

Sometimes the tablets had dolls or figurines attached, and these might have their hands bound or might be mutilated. Bits of the target's hair or clothing could be included. Gager says the effects sought by the curse tablets were many, all of them bad: "[They] included] death, illness . . . loss of memory, various forms of mental suffering, sleeplessness, involuntary celibacy, loss of family and house, public humiliation, defeat in war and athletic competition, failure in business, conviction in public courts, denial of an afterlife, and general lack of success."

The sinister nature of these invocations of evil is relieved somewhat by the fact that one of their most common uses in Roman times was by bettors seeking to defeat an opposing horse in a race or to prevail in other athletic competitions. Faraone notes a third-century Athenian curse against a wrestler, asking that he be rendered "deaf, dumb, mindless, harmless."

Curse tablets were also used in efforts to win a loved one's heart or to defeat a rival suitor. In these cases, the authors could be rather explicit. A love tablet from fifth-century Egypt is passionate with Theon's desire for Euphemia:

> *Let her not be able to sleep for the entire night, but lead her until she comes to his feet, loving him with a frenzied love, with affection and with sexual intercourse. For I have bound her brain and hands and viscera and genitals and heart for the love of me, Theon.*

Even more graphic is another from Egypt, dated to the second or third century, in which one Ammonion seems vehement in his desire for the fair Theodotis:

> *I bind you, Theodotis . . . by the tail of the snake, the mouth of the crocodile, the horns of the ram, the poison of*

the asp, the hairs of the cat and the penis of the god so that
you may never be able to sleep with any other man, nor be
screwed, nor be taken anally, nor fellate, nor find pleasure
with any other man but me.

Perhaps fearing that the gods don't quite get his point, Ammonion goes on to ask that "Theodotis be rendered subservient, obedient, eager, flying through the air seeking after Ammonion . . . and bring her thigh close to his, her genitals close to his, in unending intercourse for all the time of her life."

So much for foreplay. Other common, if less riveting, uses of *defixiones* were to seek vengeance upon thieves and to beat competitors in business. A third-century B.C.E. Sicilian tablet reads: "I bind the workshops of these men . . . so that they may not be productive but be idle and without luck."

Another function: defeating an adversary in a legal dispute, as in a Greek tablet from around 300 B.C.E. Of his opponents, the client says: "If they lay any counterclaim before the arbitrator or the court, let them seem to be of no account, either in word or in deed."

A related form of written cursing that thrived throughout the ancient world was tombstone curses. J. H. M. Strubbe of the University of Leiden cites a seventh-century B.C.E. inscription that seeks this for anyone defacing the grave: "May Sahar and Shamash and Nikkal and Nusk pluck your name and your place out of life, and an evil death make you die; and may they cause your seed to perish."

You might not know who Sahar and his (her?) colleagues are, and you might not want to hang around and find out. Another example, from Cilicia in Asia Minor, reads: "If anyone does any harm to the statue, may he leave orphaned children, a bereaved estate and a desolate home behind him. May he lose all his goods by fire and die at the hands of evil men."

And of course there's the familiar tombstone curse of William Shakespeare:

> *Good friend for Jesus sake forbeare*
> *To digge the dust enclosed here!*
> *Bleste be the man that spares these stones*
> *And curst be he that moves my bones.*

Strubbe notes that in the ancient world wronged people often employed curses when recourse to human law was futile or even dangerous. Tombstone curses, he adds, "must have been regarded as very powerful, since they were the wish of the dying or the dead."

Yet another common form of written curse was the "book curse," usually inscribed at the end of a book or other substantial document—precious, labor-intensive products in those days. Some called evil down upon a person who would steal or deface the work. Others warned off those who would ignore it. A tenth-century land grant in England issued a warning to whoever dared ignore its content: "Let him know that on the last and fearful Day of Assembly when the trumpet of the archangel is clanging the call and bodies are leaving the foul graveyards, he will burn with Judas the committor of impious treachery."

Historians say curses often came with usage rules. Usually, an older person's curses are thought to have power against a younger person; curses of parents on children are considered especially potent. In some cultures, women's curses are greatly feared. And even religious authorities employed them. In 1656, an Amsterdam synagogue excommunicated Dutch philosopher Baruch Spinoza—for his lack of religious observance and growing affinity for Descartes—with the following words:

> *The Lord blot out his name under heaven. The Lord set him apart for destruction from all the tribes of Israel, with all the curses of the firmament which are written in the book of The Law. . . . No man shall speak to him, no man write to him, no man show him any kindness, no man stay under the same roof with him, no man come near him.*

But be careful: the Bible warns that cursing one's parents, the handicapped, a king, or God could bring death to the curser. And speaking of the Good Book, it's hard to find a more savage array of curses than in the Bible, starting with Yahweh's expulsion of Adam and Eve from the Garden. In one breath, He condemns the serpent to crawl on the ground and feed on dust for the rest of his life, and announces to Eve, "I will multiply your pains in childbearing." He then tells Adam:

> *With suffering shall you get your food from [the soil]*
> *every day of your life. . . .*
> *With sweat on your brow*
> *shall you eat your bread,*
> *until your return to the soil,*
> *as you were taken from it.*
> *For dust you are*
> *and to dust you shall return.*

The Lord didn't kid around. Indeed, the Book of Revelation, and thus the New Testament, ends with a classic book curse:

> *This is my solemn warning to all who hear the prophecies*
> *in this book: if anyone adds anything to them, God will*
> *add to him every plague mentioned in the book; if anyone*
> *cuts anything out of the prophecies in this book, God will*
> *cut off his share of the tree of life and of the holy city.*

There can be no doubt of cursing's long, widespread, and even noble history—which may be why it's so difficult to consider it genuinely evil. True, many textbook exercises involve late-night ceremonies in disagreeable places (for example, cemeteries at midnight) and with unpleasant props (rotten meat, chicken hearts, black toads, human bones, snails, sheep's ears, goat's eyes, and blood, blood, blood).

But most curses require words alone. Want to see your boss's head "burst into a hundred pieces here and now"? Wish the telemarketer who calls at 9 P.M. to "linger forever with three-headed ogres"? Want that wretch who parked across two spaces to "eat bloody food" or "become an eager eater of [human flesh]"? It's all there for the pronouncing.

Men, if some Romeo has stolen your girlfriend, you can evoke the Old Norse wish that he "shall never hence be able to become powerful in a man's nature, so to destroy the maidenhood of [insert name] or any other maiden."

Ladies, if your man has dropped you for another, here's payback, Roman style: "Let there always be tracks of strangers in your bed and may your house always be open and well-known to the lecherous."

No, cursing is not nice—even though often entertaining—and of course cannot be indulged in by those whose religions forbid it. But life isn't always nice to us; verbal pyrotechnics are sometimes just what's needed to get us through a trying episode without anybody's ending up in the emergency room. Hey, you can always lift the curse later.

Those wishing to try it out can choose from numerous Web sites that provide anonymous delivery of zingers, though few of their offerings are as creative as the *defixiones*. Their spirit is generally savvy and benign, with one Web site—in promising not to share clients' addresses—noting that "the curse of junk e-mail is far worse than any voodoo curse could be."

But if you're going to try some freelance cursing, it might be wise to show respect for current religious practices by employing deities from humanity's long, rich history of musings on the supernatural. Fortunately, modern Westerners in particular have a limitless supply of obscure or discontinued gods to choose from. How about Daramulum, son of the Australian creator god Baiame, or the subterranean, dwarflike Maahiset from Finland? There's also the Caucasus storm god Uacilla, the fertility god Xewioso from Dahomey, and the deified Sumerian king Lugalbanda. And don't forget the Slavonic sun god Dabog, the virginal Britomartis of Crete, or the equally virginal Boldogasszony, goddess of the ancient Hungarians.

Whoever you invoke, it seems clear that cursing, officially condemned as an evil pursuit without redeeming value, is in fact a universal human practice with a pedigree longer than most religions and a wide range of prized (if unproven) benefits for people's health, property, fortunes in the afterlife, and chances for hooking up this weekend. How can something be both bad and good? An awkward question, and one we must face again as we consider lying, an even more obviously evil practice that also turns out to be, well, maybe not so evil.

Still conflicted about cursing? Remember, nobody expects us to be perfect. True, Jesus told his followers, "Bless those who curse you." But then, He didn't have to take the freeway.

Nine

GOOD-BYE, JOHN WAYNE

When he lies, he speaks his native language, for he is a liar and the father of lies.

—JESUS, SPEAKING OF THE DEVIL

A liar lies to himself as well as to the gods. Lying is the origin of all evils.

—MAHARATNAKUTA SUTRA (BUDDHIST)

A little inaccuracy sometimes saves tons of explanation.

—SAKI

127

None of us could live with an habitual truth-teller; but thank goodness none of us has to.

— MARK TWAIN

It's a classic scene, a genuflection before America's cherished myth of frontier honor. John Wayne rises to his feet and steps back from the table as the rowdy saloon falls silent. The tinkling piano stops. The bartenders duck. Wayne eyes the man sitting across from him and grimly utters that most fearsome of challenges: "You calling me a *liar?*"

For Hollywood, this scene is a fine excuse for a barroom brawl. For the rest of us, however, it raises an intriguing question: had Wayne—perhaps during a recent cattle drive—been catching up on his Kant?

Not likely. Still, the saloon showdown turns out to be more than just a convenient cliché. It even, in its way, reflects a profound belief apparently shared by many cultures and dating back thousands of years: that lying is the essence of evil.

The Egyptians believed this. The towering pre-Christian Persian prophet Zarathushtra agreed; his lord of evil, Angra Mainyu, was the personification of the lie. Aristotle said, "Falsehood is in itself mean and reprehensible." St. Augustine said all lies are sins against God: "To use speech, then, for the purpose of deception . . . is a sin. Nor are we to suppose that there is any lie that is not a sin, because it is sometimes possible, by telling a lie, to do service to another."

No wiggle room there. In Dante's famous thirteenth-century epic, *The Divine Comedy,* liars were punished by being cast down into the second-lowest circle of hell (just above traitors). Kant, a giant among Western philosophers, stated that a liar "annihilates his dignity as a man," and argued that lying is *always* wrong, even, say, to protect an innocent victim from a pursuing murderer. Yes, you might end up aiding the murderer's foul deed, Kant said, but only dogged truthfulness keeps you blameless: "To be truthful in all declarations ... is a sacred and absolutely commanding decree of reason, limited by no expediency."

A bit extreme? Maybe. But remember, Yahweh himself, in Exodus, proclaimed, "Thou shall not bear false witness against thy neighbor" as one of His ten core commandments to humans. At the other end of the Bible, in Revelation, the angel tells John that among those excluded from the New Jerusalem will be "everyone of false speech and false life."

It doesn't stop there. George Washington, let's remember, could not tell a lie. Our other favorite president, Abraham Lincoln, remains "Honest Abe." Modern savants from C. S. Lewis to M. Scott Peck have focused on the lie as a key manifestation of evil. Peck even entitled his book on evil *People of the Lie,* referring to the deception some inflict upon others and themselves.

So John Wayne was right to be miffed. Lying has been famously reviled for centuries. And while that fact might be news to many of us, it somehow instantly feels right: lying is clearly, viscerally wrong. But why?

The destructive effects of lying, many thinkers have said, go well beyond merely the issuance of incorrect data or the violation of some code of polite conduct — or even the uncanny offensiveness of the local car-dealer commercial. Every lie, they say, has many victims. It attacks us all; in fact, by attacking the fundamental expectation of veracity that must exist among members of a functioning society, it gradually dissolves the glue that makes communal existence possible. If deception becomes routine, it degrades our precious human gifts of language and reason, and ultimately promotes chaos.

The philosopher Sissela Bok notes:

> *Some level of truthfulness has always been seen as essential to human society, no matter how deficient the observance of other moral principles. Even the devils themselves, as Samuel Johnson said, do not lie to one another, since the society of Hell could not subsist without truth any more than others.*

Clearly, Mr. Johnson never tried to buy a car.

So. An all-star parade of the world's greatest thinkers has pretty much decided: Lying is not merely vulgar or nasty or tolerable only in private among consenting adults. It is a foul and deadly form of evil that eats away at human goodness.

How awkward, given that, as Mark Twain put it, "everybody lies—every day; every hour; awake; asleep; in his dreams; in his joy; in his mourning; if he keeps his tongue still, his hands, his eyes, his attitude, will convey deception—and purposely."

How interesting that this despicable practice is so widespread in nature—in camouflage, in birds' faking of injury to divert predators from their nests, in various animals' techniques for making themselves look bigger and fiercer.

How odd, given that this foul habit seems equally widespread among America's captains of industry—the names Enron, WorldCom, Tyco, Global Crossing, and Arthur Andersen pop to mind—a number of whom have, over the past few years, been caught deliberately, extensively, elaborately lying.

How puzzling to find that a practice loathed by moral leaders throughout history is also one that seems a natural and sometimes even necessary part of every-day life. Indeed, psychologist Charles Ford calls it a healthy part of growing up: "Lying is . . . an essential component in the process of developing autonomy and differentiating oneself from one's parents."

Some religious fundamentalists might embrace such conclusions as further proof that we're all sinners. But it hardly helps our pursuit of evil to find that one of its classic manifestations is both bad, and, well, not bad.

Let's start with definitions. Bok notes that we must exercise care in deciding what we mean by a lie. For one thing, she notes, human communication is routinely distorted by any number of agents: "The speaker, for example, may be mistaken, inarticulate, or using a language unknown to the listener. . . . At the receiving end, deafness, fatigue, language problems, or mental retardation may affect the reception of the message."

Sounds like a White House aide explaining what the president "meant to say." In addition, Bok says, deception can be accomplished "through gesture, through disguise, by means of action or inaction, even through silence." She arrives at a working definition of a lie as "any intentionally deceptive message which is stated."

Simple enough. And "intentional deception" sounds pretty evil. But we immediately run into obvious problems. Is it evil to assure your friend that he *doesn't* look fat in that swimsuit? Or to tell a terminally ill patient how good she looks today? To confirm a child's belief in Santa Claus? To mislead a violent criminal? To deceive volunteers in a medical experiment in order to establish a control group for a potential miracle cure?

Most would say not. And, to be fair, influential thinkers like Augustine and Kant showed their awareness of this glaring problem with their absolute condemnation of lying. In the thirteenth century, the Christian theologian Thomas Aquinas refined Augustine's views by dividing up lies into those told to help another, those told in fun, and those intended to harm; all were still sins, Aquinas concluded, but only the last were serious sins. Even Kant, as a young teacher, reportedly lectured about situations in which telling untruths was permissible, though scholars apparently disagree over the reliability of these early accounts.

Socrates, in Plato's *Republic*, condemned lying as "subversive and destructive"—except when wise rulers find it necessary: "Then, it's appropriate for the rulers, if for anyone at all, to lie for the benefit of the city in cases involving enemies or citizens, while all the rest must not put their hands to anything of the sort."

It seems politics hasn't changed. Most religions' attitude towards lying seems to be one of fierce and righteous condemnation—with exceptions. Judaism, for example, permits lies in several instances, including to make peace and preserve modesty. Islam also recognizes circumstances in which deception is allowed.

But these are rare exceptions to an otherwise iron-clad ban on lying, grudgingly permitted by stern moral masters. Other thinkers have gone much further, not only accepting deception but actually embracing it. Friedrich Nietzsche said, "We need lies in order to live." Twain wrote, "No fact is more firmly established than that lying is a necessity of our circumstances—the deduction that it is then a Virtue goes without saying."

Oscar Wilde, with customary bravado, in 1889 mourned the demise of lying—the rise of "realism"—as a mortal blow to art and beauty:

> *One of the chief causes that can be assigned for the curiously commonplace character of most of the literature of our age is undoubtedly the decay of lying as an art, a science, and a social pleasure. The ancient historians gave us delightful fiction in the form of fact; the modern novelist presents us with dull facts under the guise of fiction.*

Wilde, as usual both playful and profound, feared that the late nineteenth century's "monstrous worship of facts" would lead only to contemplation of the obvious and depressing grimness of everyday reality. "Lying, the telling of beautiful untrue things, is the proper aim of Art." Lying had to be preserved—indeed, cherished—if humans were to preserve their love for beauty and their precious gift of imagination. Hopefully, Wilde added, we would return to our senses: "Society sooner or later must return to its lost leader, the cultured and fascinating liar. . . . For the aim of the liar is simply to charm, to delight, to give pleasure. He is the very basis of civilized society."

On a less flamboyant note, Marie-Louise von Franz, in her widely cited book, *Shadow and Evil in Fairy Tales,* speaks of an ancient and widespread folk tradition in which lying is the right thing to do. According to von

Franz there is an "infinite" number of old tales in which a witch or god has a secret, "dark" side to her powers that she forbids, say, a servant girl to probe into. The girl does eventually witness this tabooed aspect but repeatedly denies having done so. Finally, the witch or god *rewards* the girl for having lied to her and not having given away her or his dark side. The lesson, von Franz suggests, is that "there is a form of tactful lying about the evil or the dark side of these great divinities which is not immoral," perhaps because the witch or god is "ashamed of her darkness . . . and does not want the child to mention it."

And if all this sounds unfamiliar, it's not a flaw in your education. Von Franz said this common motif "shocked later Christian European storytellers so much that many of the modern versions transform it" to make lying always bad.

So we're still left with a monumental clash between historical and moral traditions about what Winston Churchill called "terminological inexactitude." Our dilemma is all the more critical because intentional deception so permeates today's wired and wireless America that the very air seems to crackle with lies.

Maybe the Old West was different, at least via Hollywood, but today everybody's a liar. In an age drenched in hype and spin and disinformation and irony, nobody with any sense automatically assumes anybody else is telling the truth about anything.

American popular culture wallows in perfunctory deception—in advertising and entertainment and in the lackluster falsehoods routinely uttered by our notables in government and business. Indeed, deliberate public lying is not only tolerated, it's legal. American courts have repeatedly condoned "puffery," the common term for the boasts and bombast that today seem to accompany all products and services. A January 2003 *Wall Street Journal* article noted that, legally, it doesn't matter whether Pizza Hut truly bakes "the Best Pizza Under One Roof" or Bayer produces "the World's Best Aspirin." The law, according to one legal textbook, protects "a seller's privilege to lie his head off." The rest of us cheat in school or on our taxes, inflate our resumés, exaggerate symptoms to see the doctor sooner, take false sick days from work, and so on—none of which is harmless.

Some sociological studies report that men tend to lie to make themselves look good, while women do so to make other people feel better about themselves. But we all lie.

Thus our modern mantra: "Whatever."

For a glimpse of the veracity principle at work atop American public life, consider a *New York Times* interview with former White House press secretary Mike McCurry and Liz Rosenberg, PR agent for Madonna (yes, the pairing itself is suggestive). Kant and St. Augustine spoke of lying as evil; these two came close to speaking of it as art.

McCurry, President Clinton's chief spokesman, said his job involved "the art of telling the truth slowly." Rosenberg said, "I guess there's an art to the information that you give out and you don't give out."

Not that these two powerful aides to major American celebrities hadn't reflected upon the age-old question of truth and falsehood. Clearly they had.

> ROSENBERG: *"There's no sense in not at least having a reputation for being honest."*
> McCURRY: *"[Spin] is not a lie. It's a self-interested selection of facts."*

Yeah, whatever.

True, we modern secular citizens have become more sophisticated about lying—or at least we'd like to think so. Clinton famously lied to the American people—directly, blatantly, purposefully—then did it again under oath in a formal judicial proceeding. Still he wasn't tossed out of office. This was apparently because most Americans didn't see what he lied about as being all that important; or perhaps because they saw Clinton's most vigorous prosecutors as being no better. The mere fact that America's grandest public official and putative moral leader intentionally deceived us was apparently not much of an issue. After all, it's hardly unusual.

A quarter-century earlier, another American president lied and did get tossed. Richard Nixon told a lot of lies, then piled up more and more as the earlier ones were discovered. He resigned in 1973 rather than face impeachment—an ordeal that Clinton faced and survived. Some might claim that these different outcomes reflect inherent wisdom on the part of the American people and their representatives: Nixon, after all, lied about his secret misuse of the enormous powers of government; Clinton lied about having extramarital sex on duty with a consenting, if clueless, adult.

Is that why Clinton survived? It would be heartening to think so. But it also might be simply because Clinton was a charmer, while Nixon was not. Or, even less heartening, it might be because we've grown that much more oblivious to intentional deception by our highest public figures. And, looking back, even the fact that Nixon paid the price is scant cause for cheer. Before Nixon, Lyndon Johnson lied ferociously about Vietnam; after Nixon, Jimmy Carter won the presidency pledging, "I will never lie to you," suggesting that for a while there at least we mustered up some collective outrage about official deception. But we couldn't sustain it. Ronald Reagan, generally considered very effective in office, lied repeatedly about the Iran-Contra Affair and once, bizarrely, about having helped liberate a German concentration camp in World Word II. And what was that the elder Pres. George Bush said about reading his lips?

Taking shots at double-talking politicians is easy sport. But events like the Watergate scandal coldly illustrate the corrosive effects of deception warned of by our great thinkers. Watergate, like Vietnam before it, did severe long-term damage to Americans' confidence in their highest leaders and lent tremendous power to the cynicism that prevails today. Likewise, the dilemma posed by lying remains much more than just an annoying fact of life. It just might point toward a profound truth about evil.

For one thing, the seemingly irreducible fact that lying can be both evil and not evil deals a blow to absolutist moral systems, whether Christian or communist. It nicely illustrates the maddening ambiguity at the core of our conception of evil—why five thousand years and countless brilliant religious and moral systems have failed to clear it up. For another, it strongly suggests that evil—however exactly we identify it—does not infect humans from without but springs from within the deepest recesses of their character.

Finally, the dilemma of lying might further support the wisdom of separating big-E Evil from small-e evil; that is, distinguishing ideology from act. Ideology—again, religious or otherwise—proclaims grand and immutable rules about good and evil, truth and lies, backed by some transcendent authority. Yes, grand rules can be such a comfort to us mere, stumbling humans. But they are not a comfort to those countless souls cruelly punished for violating them. Plus, every ideology seems so often to have to scramble to back up and qualify itself in the face of everyday life. This is useful?

Viewing evil simply as individual acts, on the other hand, seems a better way to separate lying from what we might call benign deception. And if this approach works here, might it also work across the broader good–evil range? The downside, of course, is that we're left without ideology's security blanket — its soothing, yet uplifting, explanation of why truth and falsehood even matter, beyond everyday practicality. That leaves us on our own with yet another unnerving moral knot. Nietzsche, ever on the lookout for moral knots, said: "That lying is a necessity of life is itself a part of the terrifying and problematic character of existence."

It seems all we sophisticated moderns can say with any confidence is that, in the absence of strong reasons to the contrary, it's better to speak truths than lies. Why? Well, as Bok and others note, we all benefit from living in a society in which truth is the norm, even if it's just the official norm; that is, a society in which most people pay their rightful taxes, stop at stop signs, don't cheat the office coffee fund, and tell the truth in court. So we should all do our parts to keep it so.

And if we all lied all the time, lying would lose its tactical value.

Not much grand or noble about that. So much for the real or imagined code of the Old West. Maybe it's just as well the Duke is gone.

Ten

EVIL BECOMES ANNOYING

The most dangerous [satanic] groups are the ones we know nothing about.

—CAPT. DALE GRIFFIS (RETIRED),
TIFFIN, OHIO, POLICE DEPARTMENT

This is no dream! This is really happening!

—ROSEMARY, BEING IMPREGNATED BY SATAN,
IN THE FILM *ROSEMARY'S BABY* (1968)

Master of Slanders, dispenser of the benefits of crime, Administrator of sumptuous sins and great vices, Satan, thee we adore, reasonable God, just God!

—BLACK MASS INVOCATION
IN HUYSMANS, *LA-BAS*, 1891

People need ritual, with symbols such as those you find in baseball games or church services or wars.

—ANTON LAVEY,
FOUNDER OF THE CHURCH OF SATAN

Baseball games?

The last two passages, a mere seventy-eight years apart, would seem to trace the final decline of satanism from dreadful scandal to annoying hobby. In the time of Huysmans, a celebrated French "decadent" writer, the Prince of Darkness still cut a large and ferocious figure among much of the populace. Praising Satan aloud, insulting Jesus, mocking Church ritual, ridiculing the Gospels—all that still meant something for most people. Black Masses, supposedly using a naked woman as the altar and featuring sexual acts, were—whether or not completely believed in—considered shocking—even dangerous—matters.

Then came two world wars, the Holocaust, and Hiroshima. Today we're stalked by real horrors—from global warming to Ebola to terrorism—that make dis-respecting religious artifacts in darkened rooms while sipping animal blood seem little more than a silly prank. And now we have Anton LaVey, modern Amer-ica's most infamous satanist, defending his fearsome rit-uals by evoking the Boys of Summer.

Not exactly ferocious. Yet, strangely enough, Amer-ica's obsession with satanic cults and satanic crimes has not gone away. Widespread belief in the loathsome deeds of the Prince's legions of secret followers peaked again in the 1980s and early 1990s—and apparently still maintains a grip on millions of imaginations, if not souls. Criminal satanism has survived as popular legend into the third millennium; even educated, secular-minded Americans seem hesitant to dismiss it outright. Despite a total absence of proof, belief in criminal satanism has proven remarkably resilient.

In fact, the only reasonable conclusion is that the whole belief system surrounding tales of widespread satanic crime is the result of a gigantic fraud. It's a fraud made possible by the tireless labors of many earnest people and some deceitful ones, but ultimately by our willingness to be fooled and stay fooled. What exactly are we doing here? America's crusades against supposedly satanic crime and deviance have ruined innocent lives and squandered millions in taxpayer dol-lars. True, they make great TV. But they fill peoples' minds with nonsense, provoke unnecessary fears, and promote intolerance. Nor is "crusade" too strong a word. Here is psychiatrist Dr. Bennett Braun of Chicago, once hailed nationally as a pioneer in the treatment of multiple-personality disorder: "We are working with a national-international type [satanic] organization that's got a structure somewhat similar to the Communist cell structure, where it goes from local small groups to local consuls, regional consuls, district consuls, national consuls." It's worth noting that, in 2000, Braun had his license suspended in a settlement with the state of Illinois after a woman complained that he had convinced her she'd been involved in a satanic cult. Meanwhile, a report circulated at social-work and police conferences across the country stated: "Ritual abuse has also occurred, without parents knowing, at preschools, day-care centers, churches, summer camps, and at the hands of baby-sitters and neighbors. . . . Children are subjected to sexual abuse [and] ritual intimidation to terrorize them into silence."

Finally, author Robert Hicks reports an account of day-care abuse presented to a 1988 Virginia police seminar. If nothing else, the story describes a logistical marvel:

> *Once the parents had dropped them off for the day, the day-care staff bussed the children to an airfield, loaded them onto an airplane, and then flew them to a ceremonial site. Day-care staff . . . forced the children to lie in open coffins that were then lowered into the earth. . . . The high*

priest retrieved and then sexually assaulted the children. . . .
After the rituals, the day-care staff returned the children
[by airplane] to the center, where the unsuspecting par-
ents picked them up at the end of the day.

Many such bizarre, disturbing accounts have come from seemingly authoritative official sources. Can they be true?

Actually, no.

First, let's remind ourselves of the key distinction between Satan and satanism. Whether a powerful supernatural entity devoted to evil *does* exist is of course a question beyond the reach of human reason. Further, we must be careful not to confuse satanic cults with generally peaceful religious practices such as Santeria, Voudon, and Wicca—themselves too often persecuted in the name of eradicating evil.

Fine. But whether a massive network of secret groups devoted to murder, cannibalism, and child sexual abuse does exist in America *is* susceptible to rational inquiry. And rational inquiry—by scholars, journalists, and the FBI—has repeatedly concluded in the negative.

It's not even close. In 1989, for example, FBI agent Kenneth Lanning reported that extensive research left him "unable to identify even one documented satanic murder in the United States." Lanning concluded: "After all the hype and hysteria is [sic] put aside, the realization sets in that most satanic/occult activity involves the commission of NO crimes, and that which does, usually involves the commission of relatively minor crimes."

Sociologist Jeffrey Victor, in his comprehensive 1993 study, *Satanic Panic,* called satanism "a garbage can category": "There is absolutely no evidence whatsoever for the existence of an organized network of criminals who use satanism as an ideology to justify criminal activities."

In the early 1990s the national Center on Child Abuse and Neglect sponsored a national survey of law-enforcement and health-care workers that could find no substantiated cases of organized satanic cults committing crimes against children, according to the psychologist who directed the study.

In his extensive 2000 study, *Raising the Devil,* Pennsylvania State University folklorist Bill Ellis agreed that "the ritual abuse investigations and trials of the 1980s and early 1990s represented a . . . waste of expense and needless ruin of reputations and livelihoods."

This is worth repeating. Satanism, as a widespread conspiracy promoting crime and destruction and systematically subverting social values, does not exist today in America and probably never existed anywhere.

Never. Anywhere. Ever.

So why have so many of us fervently believed in the evils of satanism? One answer lies in Western society's long tradition of demonological scapegoating.

It's a time-honored practice. The ancient Greeks accused the Jews of ritual abuse and mutilation of abducted children, as Debbie Nathan and Michael Snedeker note in their book, *Satan's Silence*. Centuries later, the Romans charged Christians with sacrificing infants and holding orgies. In medieval Europe, Christians took their turn accusing Jews of ritualistically murdering Christian infants—the notorious "blood libel" myth, which still lingers. The Christians also began investigating witchcraft, as reflected in the widely circulated tenth-century *Canon Episcopi*, which directed bishops to look into local rumors about women and magic. Some scholars say our modern myth was launched in 1022, with the execution of a group of French heretics caught in a local power dispute. "The satanic cult legend that one hears repeated today was born in Orleans in the eleventh century," Jeffrey Victor writes.

In the thirteenth century, the Cathar heretics of southern France—who practiced a form of Gnosticism—were accused by the Vatican of devil-worship; they were executed en masse in the early stages of the Inquisition. In the thirteenth century the infamous German inquisitor Conrad of Marburg claimed to have uncovered and eliminated many satanists. Although Conrad was murdered in 1233, Pope Gregory IX officially approved of his deeds that same year. "The Papacy thus gave its official imprimatur," historian Jeffrey Richards writes, ". . . to the whole Satanist paraphernalia of secret meetings, appearances by the Devil, obscene initiation rites, and bisexual orgies." In the fourteenth century Europe's wealthy and powerful Knights Templar organization was accused of satanism, orgies, roasting of infants, and other nasty acts by the French king Philip IV, who smashed the group and confiscated its wealth. Indeed, historians note that denunciations of rivals as satanists were frequent tactics employed in the intrigue that occupied the more bored and imaginative members of Europe's royal courts. Even popes themselves were not immune, with Pope Sylvester II and Pope Gregory VII being accused of consorting with the Devil; Philip IV of France charged Pope Boniface VIII and Bishop Guichard of Troyes with the same crime.

The bloody European witch craze of the sixteenth and seventeenth centuries portrayed its quarry as existing all over Europe and as being united in a vast conspiracy headed by Satan. Their supposed practices were identical to those that figure in accounts of witchcraft today: nighttime ceremonies ("sabbats"), rituals mocking the Mass, sexual orgies, denunciations of Christianity, drinking of blood, and sacrifice of children. Pious imaginations ran wild. Thousands, mostly women, were persecuted, tried, tortured, and murdered. The Roman Catholic Church's official fifteenth-century witch-hunting handbook, *Malleus Maleficarum (The Hammer of*

Witches), contains the confession of a typical "witch" about rituals routinely performed with dead infants.

> *Then we secretly take them from their graves, and cook them in a cauldron, until the whole flesh comes away from the bones to make a soup which may easily be drunk. Of the more solid matter we make an unguent which is of virtue to help us in our arts and pleasures and our transportations.*

The seemingly universal hysteria about satanism and witchcraft was further fueled by King James I of England, famous for sponsorship of a new translation of the Bible in 1611. James was also an avid believer in satanism, and published his *Demonologie* to prove that "the assautes of Sathan are most certainly practized, & that the instrumentes thereof, merits most severly to be punished." The late seventeenth century witnessed a Parisian scandal that Gareth Medway, in his book *Lure of the Sinister*, cites as one of the few verifiable instances of "black magic" rituals that live up—almost—to centuries-old folklore. This was the Chambre Ardente Affair of 1678, in which several high-society fortune-tellers were arrested and convicted of practicing abortion and furnishing poison to unhappy wives. One of them reportedly had a secret furnace in her house for burning fetuses. An elderly priest named Abbé Guibourg later confessed that he'd been paid by a Madame de

Montespan to conduct mock masses on the belly of a woman, with intonations to "Astaroth" and "Asmodee" and using the blood and entrails of a dead fetus. Guibourg also said he'd consecrated a mixture of sexual fluids and bat's blood for use as a magic charm.

Unpleasant, yes, but diabolical? Alas, not quite. Medway says the goal of these repellent undertakings was apparently not the triumph of Satan or the overthrow of Christianity. It was to magically secure the romantic attentions of the king for Madame de Montespan.

In the nineteenth century, a former French cleric named Eliphas Levi wrote books portraying Satan as a positive spiritual force. These books appealed to young French poets and gentlemen celebrating "decadence" out of opposition to that era's smug belief in the triumph of reason and progress. One of the more celebrated satanic books was *La-Bas (Down There)*, published in 1891 by J. K. Huysmans. A novel, the book purported to contain authentic descriptions of a Black Mass and other occult practices in late-nineteenth-century Paris. Its characters spoke confidently of an international satanist organization "which rules America and Europe, like the curia of a pope." One of the main characters, Des Hermies, also voices the Decadents' theme of satanism as a heroic stance: " 'Since it is difficult to be a saint,' said Des Hermies, 'there is nothing for it but to be a satanist. One of the two extremes. Execration of impotence, hatred of the mediocre, that, perhaps is one of the more indulgent definitions of Diabolism.' "

Fast-forward to the 1960s: In hindsight, it's easy to see why America was ripe for a revival of what Jeffrey Victor called "satanic panic." Driven by a mix of longing and lunacy, those years saw an explosion of "alternative" spiritual practices, including those based on ancient pagan or Oriental religions. This spectacle became linked in the popular imagination with a series of disturbing events, from riots, protests, recreational drug use, and youthful rebellion to the Manson gang murders and the 1978 mass suicide at the People's Temple in Guyana.

In 1974 spooky reports started airing about ritualistic cattle mutilations in the American West; the accounts persisted, even though the cases were later attributed to snakebite, predators, and disease. A 1989 Texas newspaper article quoted a police "expert" relating signs of satanic mutilation: "Look for absence of blood. There will be absolutely none. That is accomplished by first killing the animal, perhaps, by shooting coolant down its throat. Then, using a stolen blood pump, they actually suck the blood out."

Adding to the hysteria—and capitalizing on it—was the founding of the Church of Satan in 1966 by Anton Szandor LaVey, a former carnival worker and photographer interested in magic and the occult. Buoyed by the superheated atmosphere of San Francisco, LaVey's relentlessly self-promoting operation, headquartered in his black-painted house, claimed Hollywood celebrities as members, performed satanic baptisms and marriages, provided dramatic quotes to eager reporters, and—did little else. As noted in his *Satanic Bible,* LaVey *opposed* physical violence against others and argued instead for a sort of aggressive hedonism freed of Christianity's stifling strictures against sex and other pleasures of the flesh. LaVey's "Nine Satanic Statements" do embrace vengeance, indulgence, and "physical, mental, or emotional gratification." At the same time, however, they celebrate such values as "vital existence," "undefiled wisdom," and "kindness to those who deserve it."

LaVey, who did a cameo turn in *Rosemary's Baby* as, of course, the Devil, flourished for a couple of years in the warm glow of indiscriminate publicity. By the early 1970s, however, he had fallen out with many of his followers and ceased public rituals. In part, this was because even LaVey had had enough of satanists:

> It became rather embarrassing after awhile. I'd step off the plane and there they'd be, all huddled together to meet me in their black velvet robes with huge Baphomets [medallions] around their necks. . . . I was trying to present a cultured, mannered image and their idea of protest or shock was to wear their "lodge regalia" into the nearest Denny's.

A splinter group founded the Temple of Set in 1974. Neither organization has apparently ever had more than a few thousand official members, and—despite zealous scrutiny by antisatanists—neither has ever been implicated in any crime.

Yet satanic crimes abound—at least in the minds of millions of believers.

- A 1989 law-enforcement conference in New Hampshire declared that there were over 2 million members of satanic cults in the United States, and that many unsolved kidnappings and serial murders were their doing.
- A 1990 California State publication related similar claims by experts, including Dr. Braun, who estimated that up to fifty thousand Americans "could be victims of Satanic Ritual Abuse."
- Evangelist Jerry Johnson, in a 1989 book, cited a Utah prison official as estimating that "between 40,000 and 60,000 human beings are killed through ritual homcides in the United States each year."
- Child advocate Kenneth Wooden declared in 1988 that "25 percent of all unsolved murders are ritualistic in nature and the victims are children and women."
- In a 1992 medical seminar, a Dr. D. Cory Hammond presented "independently confirmed"

information about how the U.S. government secretly brought "satanist/Nazi doctors" to America after World War II to help develop brainwashing techniques; "they did—and do—practice on children, who are programmed to commit sexual acts then forget about them."

- In his 1999 Book of Spiritual Warfare, Denver-based evangelist Bob Larson warned that "hundreds of bizarre cults operate secretly," and he repeated anew the familiar lore: "Human sacrifice among current satanic cults is often well organized and extremely efficient. Anticoagulants are used to store blood drained from a body, which may be disposed of in a portable crematorium."

Murder, child kidnapping and molestation, suicide pacts, grave robbing, animal mutilation, cannibalism, pornography, and orgies—all in the name of Satan. Behind these horrors, it was claimed, lurked a national or international conspiracy of satanists, including many wealthy and powerful figures; such claims were solemnly repeated on TV and radio talk shows and by police and civic groups. Many churches, especially fundamentalist Christian churches, busily fanned the fears.

Clerical and law-enforcement "experts" developed elaborate "cult crime models" that divided up America's teeming mass of secret satanists into transgenerational family practitioners, organized (public) satanists, self-styled satanists, and dabblers. They responded to the glaring lack of evidence by postulating a "hidden" uppermost level of satanic power and control that engineered the conspiracy of silence and quashed efforts to reveal the truth.

LaVey's view? "There are no categories of satanists—there are satanists and nuts."

The media, of course, proved eager to chronicle people's concerns and accusations, however outlandish. Individuals began coming forward and identifying themselves as "survivors" of childhood satanic abuse, probably the most famous being the subject of the 1980 bestseller *Michelle Remembers*. The book is a first-person account by a Canadian woman of the grotesque ritual abuse she suffered as a young child at the hands of a satanic cult. At five years of age, the book claims, Michelle was repeatedly raped and sodomized, and forced to watch others being murdered and conscripted for a variety of sacrilegious rituals; she even witnessed an appearance by the Devil himself. Then she repressed these terrible memories for twenty years, remembering them only after entering therapy with psychiatrist Lawrence Pazder, who later became her coauthor and husband. *Michelle Remembers* became popular despite the remarkable fact that no evidence was found to support Michelle's claims. Repeated investigations by outsiders found nothing; Michelle's two sisters and her father denied the story, as did childhood neighbors and school-teachers in Victoria, British Columbia. There are no records of medical treatment for the numerous severe injuries she claimed to have suffered.

Still, Michelle and Pazder became sought-after "experts" on the TV talk-show circuit, which—along with books, magazines, newspapers, and Christian radio programs—were humming with satanic themes in the 1980s. *Geraldo, Sally Jesse Raphael,* and *Oprah* broadcast shows with titles like "Satanic Breeders: Babies for Sacrifice," "Satan's Black Market: Sex Slaves, Porno, and Drugs," and "Devil Babies."

Children, our icons of innocence, have been cited throughout history as especially prized victims of satanism, and the modern American version is no different. Again, it seemed to make little difference that no concrete evidence of satanic crimes—for example, thousands of missing children—could be found. Indeed, in 1999 Bob Larson issued this challenge to doubters: "Bring me the body of Jimmy Hoffa. If organized crime could kill a notable person like Hoffa . . . and leave no trace of his body, why couldn't satanic cults aided by supernatural evil forces do the same?"

Interestingly, some historians speculate that the dearth of outspoken criticism in the past may have been due in part to the fact that some social activists saw benefit in this renewed emphasis on children's welfare. As Debbie Nathan and others point out, those seeking to address such genuine and neglected ills as child abuse, sexual abuse, incest, the oppression of women, pornography, and mental illness sometimes tolerated anticult crusaders' efforts to "protect" children in a world gone demonically wrong. But of course things got out of hand. The extent of the hysteria was reflected in the infamous McMartin Preschool trial, often cited as the nation's longest and costliest criminal trial. In 1983, staff members of the Manhattan Beach, California, preschool were accused, arrested, and in some cases jailed after a woman told police that her toddler son, a McMartin student, had been sodomized. In the ensuing furor, seven people were arrested on 135 charges after numerous children—later determined to have been prompted by interviewers—gave accounts of satanic rituals and animal mutilations. By 1990, after two mistrials, all charges had been dropped against all defendants, some of whom had spent years in prison.

Subsequent investigation, Nathan says, found that children's testimony became damning only after "intense and relentless insistence by adults." What they uttered in fact were "juvenile renderings of grown-ups' anxieties."

Various writers have linked Americans' modern belief in satanism to general social stress and anxiety, loss of trust in public institutions, yearning for stable values, and need for scapegoats. Certainly any sober evaluation of America's satanic panic must conclude that it reveals less about evil than it does about our frustration and fear over how to address life's misfortunes. It makes clear that many of us need to believe in widespread satanic crimes for the same reason that we need scary movies: because just beneath the surface fright dwells a profoundly reassuring sense of security.

It's a simple formula: if we believe that massive satanic criminal conspiracies exist, we're all but accepting that Satan himself exists — which is backdoor confirmation that God exists. As a bonus, our dull, everyday miseries and squabbles magically morph into episodes of an eternal cosmic melodrama of good versus evil. The point: it's preferable to believe in something than to believe in nothing at all. Especially as we're also guaranteed by Scripture that, in the end, good will triumph and Satan will lose. Anyone bothering to glance through *The Satanic Bible* would find the same observation: "Satan has been the best friend the church has ever had, as he has kept it in business all these years."

The Prince of Darkness himself may or may not exist. But look around: real evildoers tend not to waste their time on costumes, chants, made-up rituals, and exsanguinated cows. Probably the rest of us shouldn't either.

Eleven

EVER SINCE EVE

When a woman thinks alone, she thinks evil.

—*MALLEUS MALEFICARUM*, 1486

He who lived well during his appointed time [on earth]
was to return and dwell in his native star, and there he
would have a blessed and congenial existence. But if he
failed in attaining this, at the second birth he would
pass into a woman.

—PLATO, *TIMAEUS*

*There is a good principle which created order, light, and
man, and an evil principle which created chaos, darkness,
and woman.*

—PYTHAGORAS

The Bible says that Yahweh told Moses a goat must
be sent to the fearsome demon Azazel to atone for
the evil Israel had done. Before dispatching it, however,
Aaron was to lay his hands on the goat's head and con-
fess all the community's sins, which the beast would
then bear away into the desert.

It sounded easy. It *is* easy. Which may be why
scapegoating has been such a prized way of dealing
with evil since well before Aaron, or even Azazel.

But forget goats. Our true masterwork of scapegoating, maybe even our most successful overall achievement
concerning evil, is how effectively one half of us has
used evil as a weapon against the other. Openly, relentlessly, often brutally, human males have forever demo-
nized females—as devouring fiends, as bloodsuckers,
as seductive but poisonous beauties who must be con-
trolled and punished, as creatures both helplessly possessed by evil and dangerously charged with it. This is
not just about opposing feminist policies or ridiculing
their advocates as "feminazis." This is about damning all
human females from birth as evil and corrupting creatures of Satan. Oddly enough—or perhaps not so

oddly—most men tend to deny this nasty history, or to downplay its enormous significance. Some even do so in full knowledge of how in many places today women are still treated as little better than slaves.

Maybe they'd think again if they noted this commentary on the fair sex in the infamous *Malleus Maleficarum*, the fifteenth-century German manual on witchcraft, whose use was officially backed by Pope Innocent VIII and Emperor Maximilian I: "What else is woman but a foe to friendship, an unescapable punishment, a necessary evil, a natural temptation, a desirable calamity, a domestic danger, a delectable detriment, an evil of nature, painted with fair colors!"

This, from the West's highest religious and political authority. So how did anybody come to believe such idiocy?

It began well before the fifteenth century, or Christianity. The ancient Greeks, those revered fathers of Western Civilization, believed that Pandora, the first woman, was responsible for bringing evil and misery into the world. In fact, Pandora was sent to earth by Zeus specifically as punishment for Prometheus's theft of fire from the gods. It wasn't, in other words, that Pandora simply went bad or gave in to evil; she, the first woman, was created to *be* evil. By the way, her box was actually a jar.

Pandora was far from the only evil female haunting Greek mythology. The Erinyes—known by the Romans as the Furies—were goddesses of vengeance who lived in the underworld. One of them, Alecto ("Unceasing in Anger") was summoned by Juno against Aeneas in Virgil's *Aeneid*. The Lamia was a female demon who devoured children and used her beauty to seduce young men, then to eat them too. Medusa was a vicious, fanged Gorgon who wore a mane of poisonous snakes and wielded a gaze that would turn an onlooker to stone.

Next, consider that other foundation stone of Western society, the Old Testament. "Adam and Eve in the Garden" sounds homey enough, except that this story is a vicious slur against women and no less than a divine certification of all females as evil. Eve—weak, scheming, seductive—condemns the entire human race forever by giving in to temptation, then compounds her foul deed by leading her man astray.

That's what you get for trusting a woman, as John Milton put it in *Paradise Lost* (1667), a work of immense and lasting influence:

> *Thus it shall befall*
> *Him who, to worth in women overtrusting,*
> *Lets her will rule.*

Later, Milton even has Adam call Eve "as false and hateful" as Satan himself, and to imagine perfection as a world without women:

O why did God,
Creator wise, that peopled highest Heaven
With spirits masculine . . . not fill the world at once
With men, as Angels without feminine,
Or find some other way to generate
Mankind?

Beyond Genesis, the Bible overflows with passages demonizing women. Solomon's wives famously led him to ruin. Jezebel damaged Israel by promoting disloyalty to Yahweh. Delilah seduced and destroyed Samson. Salome danced for the head of John the Baptist. Proverbs notes how a woman can seduce men with her "persistent coaxing" and her "seductive patter." Ezekiel condemns Israel for unfaithfulness by comparing it—not to a traitorous comrade—but to a woman who has "piled whoring upon whoring."

In fact, some historians see the mythological crusade to demonize women reflected in the historical clash between male gods of the hunt and female gods of agriculture. Genesis and other parts of the Old Testament are said to mirror the struggle in Palestine between the proponents of Yahweh and those of the Canaanite god Baal, son of the Great Goddess known as Asherah or Ishtar and also by several other names.

Interestingly, one of Baal's common manifestations was as a serpent. Apparently serpents figured prominently in ancient goddess religions. For these creeds, they were a force for good and symbolized wisdom or fertility or creativity or prophecy. Statutes of ancient goddesses sometimes featured snakes entwined around the deities.

All that ended, of course, at the Garden of Eden, where the author of Genesis had the serpent betray Eve and where Yahweh decreed "enmity between you [the serpent] and the woman and between your seed and her seed." Later Christian images have the Virgin Mary, the paragon of female virtue, crushing the serpent beneath her feet.

The early Christian fathers briskly carried on this tradition. Tertullian, a second-century theologian in northern Africa and an important figure in the development of Christian society, delivered a view of women that deserves to be quoted at length:

> *Don't you know that each of you is Eve? . . . You are the Devil's gateway. You are the unsealer of that forbidden tree. You are the first deserter of the divine Law. You are she who persuaded him whom the Devil was not valiant enough to attack. You destroyed so easily God's image, man. On account of your desert, that is death, even the Son of God had to die.*

Women's weapon, of course, was what St. Anselm, archbishop of Canterbury, called the "evil above all other evils . . . sexual desire, carnal delight, the storm of lust that has smashed and battered my unhappy soul." These Christian leaders were not preaching in a vacuum. Ever since Plato and Aristotle, Western philosophy has—like Western religion—tended to prize "spirit" and "mind" over "nature" and "body." The former have traditionally been associated with the male, the latter with you-know-who. In the fifth century Augustine reinforced the tradition, placing woman firmly below man in the cosmic hierarchy. Concerning Augustine's views philosopher Nel Noddings writes: "Man and things of the spirit are above the line. . . . Woman and material things are on the 'wrong,' or corporeal, side and hence represent a dreadful temptation that man must fear and avoid."

Even before religion or philosophy, humans created myths and taboos concerning menstruation and menstrual blood. We've seen that historian Paul Ricoeur has identified defilement as among humans' earliest notions of evil. Noddings and others note how this is reflected in the view of women's bodies—captives to the cycles of nature—as vessels of evil. Many writers have reported on primitive beliefs that menstrual blood and the menstruating woman herself were not only attractive to demons but also dangerous to males' strength, hunting skill, and warrior power.

Even properly married women have been suspect. Historian Allison Coudert notes that "the notion that

wives were devious and dangerous was . . . a commonplace throughout Europe before the Reformation." So
too, Coudert notes, was wife-beating, a remedy for
domestic discord commonly recommended by popular
broadsheets. Historian Jeffrey Richards notes that wife-
beating was allowed by Church law and "took place at
every level of society." Coudert writes that it was also
openly sanctioned by civil law, in some countries even to
the point of death. "Wife-beating was so common in
sixteenth-century London that civic regulations forbade
it after nine in the evening because of the noise."

From the fifteenth to seventeenth centuries, men's
need to control and punish women for their evil nature
boiled over into the European "witch craze," which has
been termed "one of the longest and most bizarre delusions in Western history." Long, bizarre, and savage: at
least tens of thousands of women—and perhaps many
more—were arrested, imprisoned, racked, scalded,
slashed, torn apart, drowned, hanged, and, of course,
burned.

Such savagery received official sanction at the highest levels in 1486 with the issuance of *Malleus Maleficarum,* surely among the most vicious books ever
published. *Malleus,* a handbook for detecting and pun-
ishing witches, had gone through twenty-eight editions
by 1600 and for a time was second only to the Bible in
influence.

In offering guidance to prosecutors, the book states that "the greatest heresy is not to believe in witchcraft"; that witches reveal their guilt by denying that they are witches; that torture is not only permitted but encouraged; and that inquisitors may use false promises of leniency to persuade suspects to admit their guilt. But *Malleus* was not just a handbook for inquisitors. It was a wholesale assault on the female sex. Most witches are women, *Malleus* informs us, because women are more credulous than men, more impressionable, "feebler both in mind and body," and "are intellectually like children."

And in the background, always, lurks women's link to evil through their bodies:

> *But the natural reason [woman is evil] is that she is more carnal than a man, as is clear from her many carnal abominations. And it should be noted that there was a defect in the formation of the first woman, since she was formed from a bent rib . . . and since through this defect she is an imperfect animal, she always deceives.*

Even that celebrated historian of superstition Jules Michelet, writing in the nineteenth century, only partially disowned this time-honored association of women and evil. In his *Satanism and Witchcraft*, Michelet did call the authors of *Malleus* "imbecile monks," and term the witch "the standing martyr of the Middle Ages."

But Michelet himself writes this of woman: "By the fineness of her intuitions, the cunning of her wiles — often fantastic, often beneficent — she is a Witch." He also suggests that the medieval Black Mass was primarily a vehicle for repressed women to strike back at established order, a "redemption of Eve from the curse Christianity had laid upon her."

Nor did men's need to demonize women end with the coming of the eighteenth-century Enlightenment or even with the arrival of Darwinism in the nineteenth century. In his fascinating book, *Idols of Perversity*, Bram Dijkstra argues that male artists and intellectuals of late-nineteenth-century Europe and America took scientific advances as simply further evidence of their ancient view of most woman as evil: "It is clear that by 1900 writers and painters, scientists and critics . . . had been indoctrinated to regard all women who no longer conformed to the image of the household nun as vicious, bestial creatures . . . creatures who were, in fact, the personification of witchery and evil."

It's a discouraging history, this wholesale persecution in the name of the highest spiritual motives. But it's also a rich one for our pursuit of evil, for man's age-old demonization of women fairly runneth over with examples of how wickedness so often springs from the fight against wickedness.

For one thing, it displays the mechanism of scapegoating at its most blatant. By blaming women for everything from Original Sin to misplacing the TV remote, males have permitted themselves to shrug off much blame and to maintain the blissful illusion that evil is something apart from them rather than within them. (Repeat after me: "It was Eve's fault.")

For another thing, the repression of women is almost a textbook case of what psychoanalysts call "projection," a process by which individuals blame others for traits they secretly loathe in themselves. Are women by nature really weak, dirty, lustful liars?

A related insight is how we demonize things we cannot control. Men like St. Anslem have long anguished over their inability to control their deepest physical urges, the impulses that arise from the animal nature that Christians and others have sought to suppress if not completely deny. Women's bodies are of course the object of these passions. But what powerful force could be lurking in the background, foiling men's noble efforts to attain and preserve sexual purity? Must be the Devil.

On the other hand, man's domination of women shows how we perpetuate evil by trying to use it as a tool of control. Clerics approvingly quoted the biblical admonition in Samuel that "rebellion is as the sin of witchcraft." Coudert, among others, notes that the witch craze tended to fall heaviest on women with attitude: "The women who were the most likely candidates for witchcraft accusations were also women who did not fit masculine stereotypes of the good woman as the obedient, silent, and submissive wife and mother, dependent on male kin."

The sheer magnitude of this historical record suggests we might rethink our basic approach to evil. One compelling direction is offered by Noddings, who argues that our Western morality is powered by a masculine dynamic of what she calls "ethical terror." This "posits a threatening parent or deity who may impose suffering for a mistake, transgression, or even a bit of misfortune." Instead, Noddings maintains, we could nurture a dynamic of "ethical concern," which is "a recognition that natural evil threatens all of us and that we should therefore band together lovingly to offer aid and comfort."

While much too complex to ponder here, this ideal certainly sounds worth striving for. It would of course present a tremendous challenge; but if we don't succeed, we'll know who to blame.

Twelve

THE GOOD
NEWS

The sad truth is that most evil is done by people who never make up their minds to be either good or evil.

—HANNAH ARENDT

Suppose the world were only one of God's jokes, would you work any the less to make it a good joke instead of a bad one?

—GEORGE BERNARD SHAW

To ignore evil is to become an accomplice to it.

— MARTIN LUTHER KING JR.

Rape, repression, madness, torture, genocide. When we are pondering evil, the good news doesn't exactly jump off the page. Now comes another entry: failure. Our efforts to get a grip on evil have clearly fallen short. The answers we've encountered have been too few (why *did* Yahweh torture Job?) and too many (*how* many Hindu gods are there?); but most often they've simply led to more questions. Why do psychopaths exist? Could rape really be a selected survival mechanism? Can God forgive even Satan? And so on, and on, for the past eleven chapters and five thousand years. Seven centuries ago Thomas Aquinas called the philosophical Problem of Evil the greatest test of religious faith. Our little review finds that trying to explain evil is a daunting test of reason.

Does evil even exist? Here we may have made a little progress, if only by separating the big-E from the little-e form of the concept. Those who reject any use of the term *evil* can't deny that people commonly do very bad things to other people. Why shouldn't we call such behavior "evil"—in the little-e sense? That's easy enough.

The bigger question is not so easy: Does big-E Evil exist? Is there actually some mysterious, supernatural power "out there," independent of individuals yet seeking to control them? Remember that philosopher Paul Ricoeur said early humans conceived of evil as a "substance-force" that works invisibly and "infects as a sort of filth." Many of the world's religions have offered similar models. Is this right?

Most of us think so. Our most popular answer to evil has long been a purely wicked Satan who is held in check by a purely good (and, luckily, more powerful) god. Still, this is just the latest of many supernatural answers. Honestly, what are we to make of all these rudely clashing religious truths? They can't all be right. And then there's the mean fact that religion is itself a favorite excuse for inflicting evil, up to and including the latest bloody headlines.

On the secular side, a strictly rational answer to the question of big-E Evil's existence would be: not likely. Centuries of intense scrutiny have found no concrete evidence for mythological forms of big-E Evil or its fabled agents. Leviathan, along with the Loch Ness Monster, has never been reliably photographed. No one has ever really interviewed a vampire. Demons, Furies, jinns, even trolls have been damn hard to track down. All our witches have long since been murdered, along with maybe a hundred thousand possibles, just to be sure.

But science's own efforts to come up with secular versions of a universal "substance-force" have also met only partial success. True, many people are satisfied—if hardly comforted—by sociobiology's depiction of

humans as Stone Age survival machines coping poorly
with rush-hour traffic and automated telephone systems.
But don't such broad explanations risk merely substitut-
ing evolutionary psychology for, say, Calvinism? And
though the category of psychopathy may be a useful
guide through the tangled questions of mental illness and
evil, it ultimately seems to leave us with little more than a
portrait of Satan in street clothes.

Let's see. Religious belief can offer no evidence that
big-E Evil exists. Rationality cannot prove it does *not*
exist, because one cannot prove a negative. Until Satan
sits down with Barbara Walters, the best answer is:
we'll never know.

Not very satisfying. After centuries of devout faith
and fearless rationality, we're left to dwell glumly on
what we don't know. Existentialist philosopher Jean-
Paul Sartre—never a jolly type—said we heirs of the
Holocaust must admit that

> *evil is not [merely] an appearance, that knowing its cause
> does not dispel it, that it is not opposed to Good as a con-
> fused idea is to a clear one, that [it] is not the effects of
> passions which might be cured, of a fear that might be
> overcome, of a passing aberration which might be excused,
> of an ignorance which might be enlightened.*

Yet whatever it is, evil is something we cannot, in
good conscience or in naked self-interest, leave alone.

We can't give up and leave the field. To do so, as Martin Luther King Jr. notes on page 173, would be to throw in with the villains. That might be tolerable if our villains were limited to cartoon figures like Dr. Evil or Cruella Deville or even to real figures like Rasputin, who after all was just making the most of his fifteen minutes of fame. Unfortunately, our villains also include Idi Amin and Charles Manson and Gilles de Rais and Saddam Hussein and so many others who continually remind us in pain and blood that even Shakespeare's cunning Iago—like Milton's magnificent Satan—was only an actor on a stage. That evil, in the end, cannot be romanticized, trivialized, laughed off, or argued away.

Add to this the concern of people like psychologist Robert Hare, pioneer researcher of psychopathy, who feared that Western popular culture increasingly nurtures deviancy, as "some psychopathic traits— egocentricity, lack of concern for others, superficiality, style over substance, being 'cool,' manipulativeness and so forth—increasingly are tolerated or even valued."

All this suggests that getting a cognitive grip on wickedness might best be approached as a process rather than a project. Probably a lifelong process. A process unlikely to end in a flash of transcendent triumph— except for those achieving nirvana, divine visitation, or true psychopathy. But a process that, with any luck at all, can improve things a little and ease the dread. Maybe just the effort itself has some value. If we make our feelings known, it at least reminds the watching world that morality or something like it is still alive. That's a contribution. It might not rise to the level of good news, but it's something.

In chapter 1, we posited evil as extreme harm caused to innocents, in such a way that attacks our basic moral order. However stingy, this still appears useful. It might now, after hearing from Hannah Arendt, be worth noting that the extreme harm can be done "intentionally or recklessly." And, in view of the compelling arguments of evolutionary psychology, we could add that such deeds are likely "propelled by natural, biologically based aggressive tendencies."

That yields "extreme harm caused intentionally or recklessly to innocents, propelled by natural, biologically based aggressive tendencies and done in a way that attacks our basic moral order."

This is a great definition if you're getting paid by the word; otherwise, it's dutiful but overgrown. Certainly evil also must involve a shattering of human boundaries, as Joseph Conrad showed in his classic 1902 novella *Heart of Darkness*. The book—the basis for the movie *Apocalypse Now*—climaxes in a boat on the Congo River, deep in the uncharted African jungle, as the narrator observes the dying Kurtz, a mysterious trader who'd disappeared into the jungle and gradually given himself over to the temptations of absolute power:

> *I saw on that ivory face the expression of somber pride, of ruthless power, of craven terror—of an intense and hopeless despair. Did he live his life again in every detail of desire, temptation, and surrender during that supreme moment of complete knowledge? He cried in a whisper at some image, at some vision. . . .*
> *"The horror! The horror!"*

Certainly evil also bathes in the majestic sorrow of Fyodor Dostoevsky, whose character Ivan in *The Brothers Karamazov* declares that even divine harmony is not worth the price of human suffering:

> *It's not worth the tears of . . . one tortured child. . . . It's not worth it, because those tears are unatoned for. They must be atoned for, or there can be no harmony. But how? How are you going to atone for them? Is it possible? By their being avenged? But what do I care for avenging them? What do I care for a hell for oppressors? What good can hell do, since those children have already been tortured?*

In the face of such brilliant despair, suggesting that there could be good news about evil might seem monstrous. Yet there is good news.

Evil, excluding ordinary human cussedness, seems

to be the exception, if barely, in human behavior. Philosopher John Kekes says that "moral idiots" may abound, but "moral monsters" are few.

Evil in its worst forms is widely recognized and condemned. Across cultures, religions, and ethnic divides, there runs a kind of baseline of evil that most people most of the time agree should not be crossed. Regardless of ideology, few humans will endorse, say, the torture of children.

There is some justice. Despite the grievous flaws in the American criminal-justice system, for example, many real criminals are indeed punished—or at least detained, disrupted, and warned off; many wrongs are righted or at least avenged.

Evil often can be resisted or mitigated. Even without Buffy around, we are not always helpless against it. It wasn't that long ago, for example, that lynching was a popular public entertainment. The embedded bureaucratic evil noted by Arendt poses another challenge.

A lot of evil people are stupid, ignorant, and unlucky. We tend to focus successful villains like Ted Bundy and Pol Pot for good reason: they're the exceptions. This is also why most conspiracy theories, however appealing, are false; the bad guys are seldom that clever. If history forces us to conclude that God does not protect the good among us, the upside is that the evil have no special powers either.

Even the most fearful among us can take comfort in

the fact that evil will never triumph completely. All conceptions of wickedness include a limit to its growth and dominance. Christianity, Islam, and Judaism assure us that even Satan is doomed to failure. Hinduism and Buddhism are founded on a concept of balance in which evil—if more than mere illusion anyway—never disappears yet also never conquers all. Even psychopaths retain some human feelings and failings. And even ardent sociobiologists recognize that nature demands cooperation as well as conflict.

Finally, we can't avoid concluding that evil is not all bad. We like being—if not evil—at least naughty. Mae West said, "When choosing between two evils, I like to pick the one I haven't tried before." Innovation can require breaking rules. Wickedness and suffering have undeniably contributed to artistic achievement. Genius often walks arm in arm with despair. War spurs invention. Evil speaks to our urge to soar to the sun like Icarus, to transcend these mere human bounds, powered by what a satanist character in the 1891 novel *La-Bas* called our "hatred of the mediocre." What would the great bluesman Robert Johnson have left us if he grew up in Grosse Pointe? Would he still have had a hell-hound on his trail?

In fact, examining our lust for transcendence might also be the best way to understand the most fearsome of primal drives—the impulse to consciously, deliberately commit evil. Arendt might well be right in concluding that the considerable problem of intentional human evil can be traced to a virulent form of thoughtlessness. But we might also well heed Erich Fromm, Ernest Becker, and others in considering that the most fearsome evil — intentional evil — stems from a blind, yet irrepressible, human need to break loose. This, in turn, is fueled by a kind of existential rage that itself explodes forth from the cold knowledge that, though we humans have been bred to play among the planets and gaze upon eternity, we still are fated to die like any insect.

In any case evil, it appears, is part of the program. On the menu. In the manual. It might even be called the price of being human, as Fromm and others have suggested — the price of being an individual, of being a free individual. Nobody seems prepared to predict that evil will ever be completely eradicated from life on earth. It's not at all clear what would happen if evil did disappear. Would the mountaintops resound in triumph? Would the graves open? Would Elvis finally turn up?

In fact, if it's daunting to explain a world containing evil — that's our world — it's impossible to imagine a world without it. There might be a clue in that — a clue that fits well with the curious fact that, while we surely must wish that evil be abolished, we should probably, in the end, not wish too hard.

FURTHER READING

This is not a bibliography, but a list of some books I found especially helpful or otherwise memorable; I've not included such basics as the Bible, the Qur'an and other religious texts, the works of Plato, Augustine, Kant, Nietsche, Freud, and so forth, or the unending stream of news media and Internet input. Still, the hidden upside of research into a dismal topic like evil is encountering the wondrous trove of fascinating work that's out there.

One. WHERE DO WE START?

Hans Schwarz, *Evil: A Historical and Theological Perspective* (Philadelphia: Fortress Press, 1995) and Jacob Neusner, ed., *Evil & Suffering* (Cleveland: Pilgrim Press, 1998) are excellent starts—clear, concise surveys of the different ways evil has been defined and explained. Neusner focuses on the major religions while Schwarz includes psychological and sociobiological views. Amelie Oksenberg Rorty, ed., *The Many Faces of Evil* (New York: Routledge, 2001) offers a rich selection of short, original writings from St. Augustine through de Sade to the Model Penal Code. Jeffrey Burton Russell, an especially prolific and readable scholar, gives a compelling account of the history of evil in *The Prince of Darkness* (Ithaca, N.Y.: Cornell University Press, 1988), and Andrew Delbanco in *The Death of Satan* (New York: Noonday Press, 1996) gives a sweeping account of how America and the West are abandoning our once-solid belief in religion as the unimpeachable foundation of morality. It almost makes you wish Old Hairy was back. Almost.

Two. LAZARUS! COME OUT!

Many people consider the Book of Job the beginning and end of commentary on evil, and it's certainly must reading. I happen to think it paints a pretty unflattering picture of Yahweh, but that's a minority view. On a much more contemporary and human scale, Harold Kushner's small, unassuming *When Bad Things Happen to Good People* (New York: Avon, 1981) zeros in perfectly on the core question posed by evil. C. S. Lewis's *The Problem of Pain* (New York: Touchstone, 1996) is a famous and eloquent effort to reconcile evil and Christianity. Mark Larrimore offers an excellent selection of historical writings in *The Problem of Evil: A Reader* (Oxford: Blackwell Publishers, 2001), and Flannery O'Connor briefly, elegantly demolishes all smug conclusions in her story "A Good Man Is Hard to Find," in *The Complete Stories* (New York: Farrar, Straus and Giroux, 1988).

Three. THE DEVIL IN DECLINE.

It's easy to imagine that Jeffrey Burton Russell knows more about Satan than the Prince himself; in any case, Russell provides more authoritative testimony in *The Devil* (Ithaca, N.Y.: Cornell University Press, 1977). Elaine Pagels of Princeton—author of the popular *Gnostic Gospels* (New York: Vintage, 1979)—gives a fascinating account of the evolution of the Satan myth as the early Christians wielded it against each other in *The Origin of Satan* (New York: Vintage, 1995). Paul Carus's *The History of the Devil and the Idea of Evil* (New York: Gramercy, 1996) is a dated but rich survey of Satan through the ages, while *Satanism and Witchcraft*

(New York: Citadel Press, 1992) is a pleasantly spooky presentation by the famous nineteenth-century French historian Jules Michelet.

Four. SURVIVAL OF THE WORST.

For many readers, Konrad Lorenz's *On Aggression* (1963) was the first presentation of something we knew but weren't supposed to admit: We're all chock-full of natural aggression. Later, Edward O. Wilson's *Sociobiology: The New Synthesis* (Cambridge: Harvard University Press, 1975) formally threw down the academic gauntlet—though it wasn't the first work in the field, either—and sparked a sometimes vicious controversy that rages on today. Richard Dawkins's *The Selfish Gene* (Oxford: Oxford University Press, 1976) is a clear and lively account that gives an especially good exposition on genetics, while Richard Wrangham and Dale Peterson's *Demonic Males* (New York: Mariner, 1996) is a more specialized report on research about aggression in apes and, by extension, in you-know-who.

Robert Wright's *The Moral Animal* (New York: Vintage, 1994) was the clearest and most persuasive presentation on evolutionary psychology that I've seen. It's so well done that you almost don't mind concluding that all that stuff you've heard about God and salvation seems, well, pretty unlikely.

Five. POSTMODERN DEMONS.

The American Psychiatric Association's *Diagnostic and Statistical Manual of Mental Disorders*, Fourth Edition, Text Revision (Washington: American Psychiatric Press, 2000) is definitely not airport reading, but it is *the* official guidebook. It's fascinating to browse through all the categories and subcategories of mental woes—though it's worth remembering that the DSM itself has been a source of controversy, not least because for years it included homosexuality among the disorders. Robert Hare's *Without Conscience* (New York: The Guilford Press, 1993) is a straightforward introduction to psychopathy by one of the most respected authorities in the field. Numerous other works—for example, Ronald Markman and Dominick Bosco's *Alone with the Devil* (New York: Doubleday, 1989), Jonathan Pincus's *Base Instincts* (New York: Norton, 2001), and Robert Simon's *Bad Men Do What Good Men Dream* (Washington: American Psychiatric Press, 1996)—recount encounters with psychopaths by therapists and law-enforcement officials.

Six. THE MONSTER WITHIN.

Hannah Arendt's *Eichmann in Jerusalem* (New York: Viking, 1963) has been hailed and denounced for decades; I'd have to include it among the most brilliant and influential books I've ever read. Arendt wrote a number of other wonderful works as well, including *The Life of the Mind* (New York: Harcourt Brace Jovanovich, 1977), which was still in progress when she died. I won't presume to make recommendations from the vast body of Holocaust literature, except to note Gitta Sereny's *Into That Darkness* (New York: Vintage, 1983) — an interview with the former commandant of Treblinka and Sobibor — and Bernard Bergen's *The Banality of Evil* (Lanham, Md.: Rowman & Littlefield, 1998). On the subject of Eichmann himself, *Operation Eichmann* (London: Cassell, 1999) by Zvi Aharoni and Wilhelm Dietl, and *Eichmann Interrogated* (New York: DeCapo Press, 1999), edited by Jochen von Lang, are compelling and sometimes shocking accounts. Susan Neiman in *Evil in Modern Thought* (Princeton, N.J.: Princeton University Press, 2002) offers a penetrating analysis of Arendt's contribution to twentieth-century thinking about evil.

Seven. HEINOUS, CRUEL, DEPRAVED.
The justices of the U.S. Supreme Court, in *Furman v Georgia* (1972), provided a judicial review of the punishment of evil that's hard to top—especially when accompanied by all the supporting documents associated with the decision. On the other hand, prime-time TV constantly bombards us with fictionalized accounts of crime and punishment—nearly all, it seems, based on true stories. It is hard to think of a social issue that's

both more important and more relentlessly misrepresented. Many fine books have been written on the death penalty and the criminal justice system, although a high percentage can be difficult to wade through. In the end, there is no substitute in the pursuit of understanding about the course of juridical evil for personally visiting its shrine, your local courthouse.

Eight. PIGS IN YOUR CEMETERIES.
It was a delightful surprise to me to discover the wealth of literature on the topic of cursing and spells. On the hard-core academic side, Christopher Faraone produced *Ancient Greek Love Magic* (Cambridge: Harvard University Press, 1999) and, with Dirk Obbink, edited *Magika Hiera: Ancient Greek Magic and Religion* (Oxford: Oxford University Press, 1991).

And John Gager offers a dry yet still fascinating trove of information in *Curse Tablets and Binding Spells from the Ancient World* (Oxford: Oxford University Press, 1992). One cannot visit this field without considering Sir James Frazer's classic *The Golden Bough* (New York: Penguin, 1996), which—written at the dawn of the twentieth century—today reads something like an archeological find itself. On the nonacademic side there are scads of compilations, two of them being Stuart Gordon, *The Book of Spells, Hexes and Curses* (Secaucus, N.J.: Carol Publishing Group, 1997) and Leonard R.

N. Ashley, *The Complete Book of Spells, Curses and Magical Recipes* (New York: Barricade Books, 1997).

Nine. GOOD-BYE, JOHN WAYNE.

Most people looking into the topic of lying owe a lot to Sissela Bok's definitive work, *On Lying* (New York: Vintage, 1989), though it's criticized by those who believe we must cling to an absolutist standard that rejects all lying. M. Scott Peck's highly popular *People of the Lie* (New York: Touchstone, 1983) is not about lying itself but nicely shows why so many people continue to consider deception a core function of evil. Other highly readable accounts of the history and psychology of lying include Jeremy Campbell, *The Liar's Tale* (New York: Norton, 2001); David Nyberg, *The Varnished Truth* (Chicago: University of Chicago Press, 1993); and Charles Ford, *Lies! Lies! Lies! The Psychology of Deceit* (Washington: American Psychiatric Press, 1996).

Ten. EVIL BECOMES ANNOYING.

To get a quick sense of satanism taken seriously, J. K. Huysmans' *La-Bas* (New York: Dover, 1972) — first published in France in 1891 — is hard to beat. If one then jumps forward some eighty years to Anton LaVey's *The Satanic Bible* (New York: Avon, 1969), it's easy to trace satanism's fall from odious creed to marketing artifact. The revival of popular belief in — or at least publicity about — satanism has been carefully examined in excellent books such as Debbie Nathan and Michael Snedeker's *Satan's Silence* (New York: BasicBooks, 1995) and Jeffrey Victor's *Satanic Panic* (Chicago: Open Court, 1993). Gareth Medway provides a longer historical view as well as information about satanism in England in *Lure of the Sinister* (New York: New York University Press, 2001). On the other hand, a strong dose of contemporary belief in satanism can be had in Bob Larson's *Book of Spiritual Warfare* (Nashville: Thomas Nelson, 1999).

Eleven. EVER SINCE EVE.

Many books are touted as "shocking," but few I've encountered deserve it more than Heinrich Kramer and James Sprenger's *Malleus Maleficarum* (Escondido, Calif.: The Book Tree, 2000). First published in the late fifteenth century, this work—backed by both emperor and pope—functioned as Europe's official manual of persecution, torture, and murder for centuries. Packed with laughable superstitions and vicious slurs, it should be required reading for anyone who still denies our sad history of official misogyny. On a more positive note, Nel Noddings's *Woman and Evil* (Berkeley: University of California Press, 1989) offers fresh and provocative insights into man's demonization of women—as well as into the topic of evil in general—and Bram Dijkstra, in *Idols of Perversity* (New York: Oxford University Press, 1986) and *Evil Sisters* (New York: Knopf, 1996), presents stunning examples of how this demonization has been celebrated in Western art.

Twelve. THE GOOD NEWS.

John Kekes's *Facing Evil* (Princeton, N.J.: Princeton University Press, 1990) is a remarkably clear and concise modern exposition on this ancient question; you don't have to agree with all Kekes says to come away enriched by his treatment of the subject. Ernest Becker's *Escape From Evil* (New York: The Free Press, 1975) is a passionate and—I thought—extremely persuasive argument about the origins of our attitudes toward evil, as is Erich Fromm's more celebrated *The Anatomy of Human Destructiveness* (New York: Fawcett, 1975). In the end, however, it's hard to conceive of more devastating yet inspiring accounts of evil than Joseph Conrad's short, brilliant *Heart of Darkness* (New York: Penguin, 1999) and Fyodor Dostoevsky's *The Brothers Karamazov* (New York: Farrar, Straus and Giroux, 2002)—fittingly, one of the greatest novels ever written.

INDEX